THE PRACTICAL SPEECH HANDBOOK

THE PRACTICAL SPEECH HANDBOOK

Nancy Hauer
Edward Martley

National College

—

IRWIN
MIRROR PRESS
Homewood, IL 60430
Boston, MA 02116

Mirror Press: David R. Helmstadter
　　　　　　　Carla F. Tishler

Marketing manager: Lynn M. Kalanik
Project editor: Jane Lightell
Production manager: Mary Jo Parke
Designer: Mercedes Santos
Art coordinator: Mark Malloy
Illustrator: Boston Graphics, Inc.
Compositor: Impressions, A Division of Edwards Brothers, Inc.
Typeface: 10.5/13 Cochin
Printer: R. R. Donnelley & Sons Company

Library of Congress Cataloging-in-Publication Data

Hauer, Nancy
　　　The practical speech handbook / Nancy Hauer, Edward Martley.
　　　　　　p.　　　cm.
　　　Includes bibliographical references and index.
　　　ISBN 0-256-13057-4
　　　1. Oral communication.　I. Martley, Edward　II. Title
　　P95.H38　1993
　　302.2'242—dc20　　　　　　　　　　　　　　　　94–29447

Printed in the United States of America
1 2 3 4 5 6 7 8 9 0 DOC 9 8 7 6 5 4 3 2

After reviewing this book, please take a minute to give us your opinion. We appreciate your comments.

e:
k No.: BECKER SPEAK SKILL BUS CAREER
        12-4112-01   0-256-12630-5   Qty: 1

CAT   REFER   DATE   ST   SCH   PROF   SRC   O/L
 12   639456   03/02/93   40   777   028   1
s this book suitable for your course(s)?

Yes _____   PROF J KANE
                                   UNIV OF PITTS JOHNSTOWN
No _____   DEPT OF ENGLISH/BIDDLE HL

f yes, do you plan to adopt this book?   JOHNSTOWN PA 15904

Yes _____ Class size? _____

No _____

Please identify some of the features that caused you to select this text for your course(s).

.) _____

.) _____

.) _____

you have chosen not to adopt this text, please explain any deficiencies you may have encountered:

ontent _____ Comprehension Level/Too High _____

resentation _____ Comprehension Level/Too Low _____

omments: _____

_____

_____

hat book(s) are you now using in your course?

_____

_____

hy did you choose this book?

_____

_____

you have not yet adopted a textbook for your course, what is your decision date? _____

an we quote your comments? Yes ☐ No ☐

ur comments are appreciated.

e write: **Marketing Department**   Or Call: **Faculty Services**
          RICHARD D. IRWIN, INC.   **(800)-323-4560 (Continental U.S.)**
          1818 Ridge Road   **(708)-798-6000 (Outside U.S.)**
          Homewood, IL 60430

ould you be willing to discuss this questionnaire with us? If so, please indicate your phone number. _____

Fold, moisten and mail.

Meeting your needs is our business. You can help us meet these needs by sharing your opinions with us. This *IRWIN* text has been sent to you with our compliments. We hope you'll share in our enthusiasm over this excellent text. Please share your opinions with us.

 Times Mirror Books

BUSINESS REPLY MAIL

FIRST CLASS   PERMIT NO. 17   HOMEWOOD, IL

POSTAGE WILL BE PAID BY ADDRESSEE

MARKETING DEPARTMENT
RICHARD D. IRWIN, INC.
1818 Ridge Road
Homewood, IL 60430-9986

er reviewing this book, please take a minute to give us your opinion. We appreciate your comments.

No.: **HAUER PRAC SPEECH HDBK**
12-4172-01   0-256-13057-4   Qty: **1**

T   REFER   DATE   ST   SCH   PROF   SRC   O/L
2   639456   03/02/93   40   777   028   1
his book suitable for your course(s)?

s _____   PROF J KANE
                               UNIV OF PITTS JOHNSTOWN
_____   DEPT OF ENGLISH/BIDDLE HL

es, do you plan to adopt this book?   JOHNSTOWN PA 15904

s _____ Class size? _____

ase identify some of the features that caused you to select this text for your course(s).

_____

_____

_____

ou have chosen not to adopt this text, please explain any deficiencies you may have encountered:

ntent _____ Comprehension Level/Too High _____

sentation _____ Comprehension Level/Too Low _____

mments: _____

_____

_____

at book(s) are you now using in your course?

_____

_____

y did you choose this book?

_____

_____

ou have not yet adopted a textbook for your course, what is your decision date? _____

we quote your comments?   Yes ☐   No ☐

r comments are appreciated.

write: **Marketing Department**   Or Call: **Faculty Services**
         RICHARD D. IRWIN, INC.   **(800)-323-4560 (Continental U.S.)**
         1818 Ridge Road   **(708)-798-6000 (Outside U.S.)**
         Homewood, IL 60430

uld you be willing to discuss this questionnaire with us? If so, please indicate your phone number. _____

_____

Fold, moisten and mail.

Meeting your needs is our business. You can help us meet these needs by sharing your opinions with us. This **IRWIN** text has been sent to you with our compliments. We hope you'll share in our enthusiasm over this excellent text. Please share your opinions with us.

 Times Mirror
Books

Preface

➤ TO THE INSTRUCTOR:

This book is designed for use in public speaking and oral communication courses that focus on the development of practical speaking skills. A variety of approaches to courses of this type is widely practiced and, in our judgment, entirely valid. However, we have chosen to focus on those aspects of speech instruction that are of immediate value to students, both in class and when entering the workforce.

We have tried to write a friendly, personal, and concise book that will help students overcome their fear of speaking and foster confidence, rather than dwell on academic theory. Over the years, we believe our students have found this approach enjoyable, and most importantly, effective.

➤ TO THE STUDENT:

Effective speaking skills are always important for success in the classroom and in the work world. We developed this book as a guide to efficient mastery of the basic skills you need to speak before any size group, from a few friends, to a class of fellow students, to a gathering in the workplace. Above all, we want you to **use** this book—get to know the techniques and skills we and your instructors present and use them in your classes and beyond. Improving your speaking skills is a *practical* way to enhance your confidence and performance far beyond the boundaries of this course.

This book gets right down to business. The heart of effective group speaking is knowing how to meet the needs of your audience and how to organize and deliver your speech accordingly. Thus, we address these topics from the very first page. Chapter 1, "The Art of Speaking Well," Chapter 2, "Speech Basics," and Chapter 3, "Platform Manner and Delivery," set the stage for preparing and delivering basic speeches. In these chapters we briefly introduce the communication process, help you overcome stage fright, and explain how to develop your own speaking style. Chapter 4, "Discussing Speeches," covers constructive criticism in the classroom setting. We encourage you to talk with each other about your speeches. Our students have found that coaching one another is an invaluable component of a successful speech course.

These first four chapters prepare you to advance to more formal speeches. Chapters 5 through 8 offer concrete guidelines for preparing and delivering one-point, informative, demonstration, and persuasive speeches. These four categories of speeches are the building blocks of any type of speech you will deliver. You will learn how to analyze your audience and shape a speech to meet their needs and expectations, and you will master the art of directing the flow of your speech to first capture and then maintain your audiences' attention. We will show you how to use visual aids to support your speech, but most importantly, our goal is to give you the speaking confidence you need to do well in any speaking situation.

The Practical Speech Handbook also makes real connections to other aspects of your education. The final chapter, Chapter 9, "Speak Up for Yourself," explains how to put your speaking skills to work beyond speechmaking. In this chapter we offer concrete guidance on interviewing skills, effective telephone use, how to introduce a speaker, and how to accept an award. You'll learn that speaking skills are more than just classroom tools. They will serve you in your career.

Learning Objectives and Skill Builder exercises in every chapter are intended to enhance the practical, hands-on usefulness of this book:

Learning Objectives   Each chapter opens with a list of the most salient concepts explained in that chapter. These provide shared goals to work toward in learning the chapter material, and also present a preview of the chapter.

Skill Builders   These exercises close each chapter. They are interactive exercises to be performed in class, in pairs or in larger groups. Students are asked to put the chapter concepts into practice to develop and deliver brief speeches, critique each other's work, strengthen existing speechmaking skills, and develop new ones. These exercises are active reinforcers of the chapter material.

➤ ACKNOWLEDGMENTS

We'd like to thank the following reviewers for their comments and feedback during manuscript development. Their assistance was invaluable:

    Sara Fanjoy, Ontario Business College, Belleville, Ontario

    Edna Jellesed, Lane Community College, Eugene, Oregon

    Carolyn McLaughlin, Fort Lauderdale College, Fort Lauderdale, Florida

    Vincent Miskell, Metropolitan Career Institute, New York, New York

    Phyllis Riley, South Hills Business School, State College, Pennsylvania

    Celeste Toffolo, Elmira Business Institute, Elmira, New York

    Mel Wyler, Hagerstown Business College, Hagerstown, Maryland

Many thanks to the legions of shy students who, often through considerable effort, acquired speech skills that became uniquely their own. Without them, this book would not have been written.

Nancy Hauer
Edward Martley

Contents

THE PRACTICAL SPEECH HANDBOOK

THE ART OF SPEAKING WELL

By studying this chapter, you will:

- Understand the communication–
  feedback process between listener
  and speaker.

- Learn that stage fright is real,
  and most people have it.

- Be prepared to give your first
  speech.

*B*eing able to talk and liking to talk are parts of being human. Even as babies, we gurgle, coo, and howl as we attempt to communicate with those around us.

By the time we are five years old, we put forth a stream of chatter. Our parents soon develop frozen smiles and glazed eyes common to those polite souls who are subjected to an overabundance of aimless talk.

. . . .

[THE COMMUNICATION PROCESS]

This aimless talk is the beginning of the art of communication. Communication requires at least two people—a speaker and a listener; it is not a one-way process but a circular process.

The reaction of the listener provides the speaker with enough nonverbal communication (facial expression, body language, eye expression) to know what to say next.

For example, when a child asks a parent something ("Can I go out to play? Can Johnny stay overnight?"), even as he says the word, he is looking to the parent for a reaction ("Is she going to let me or not?") and is waiting for a response.

The communication process, though simple, is the same thing we call a speech. The listener may change from a parent or friend to an audience of strangers, but the process is the same.

All of us have been giving "speeches" since we began to talk. In fact, your history as a "speaker" began the instant you were born and you twisted up your face to express displeasure at leaving the comfort of the womb. The simple process of communication for each person is much the same as the baby's.

The art of communication with others is a deceptively simple process. The idea begins in the speaker's mind, is translated into words that are then projected out to the audience, heard by the audience and, if the speaker did it right, absorbed.

[LEARN TO USE EMPATHY]

The listener doesn't say anything, but the effect of the speaker's words makes him react in subtle ways to give feedback to the speaker. This is called empathy.

For example, if the speaker is relating a personal experience to an audience (one person or many), and he or she begins by describing the background facts in a serious manner, the listeners convey their acceptance of this by looking at the speaker with "listening" expressions on their faces. This communicates to the speaker that "I am listening to you; I acknowledge that I hear what you are saying."

Then, as the speaker moves further into the narrative of the story, the listeners will become aware of the humor (or other quality) of the story and they begin to react accordingly—smiling, laughing, and so forth.

Their empathy with the speaker communicates that the story is understood and appreciated. Empathy can produce very strong emotions and can be much more subtle than, say, the laughter produced by humor.

A speaker who relates a sad story to the audience can make the audience feel such strong sympathy for the speaker that waves of empathy will cause the speaker to feel deep emotion, perhaps to the point of shedding a tear. For example, a student might choose to communicate a story of his or her parents' divorce and the profound effect this had. The audience, whether or not they have been involved with divorce, will project enough empathy to recreate the speaker's original emotions.

So, we ask, if this is all so logical and natural, why can it appear so difficult?

[ACKNOWLEDGING AND CONTROLLING STAGE FRIGHT]

There come times when the human tongue ceases to wag: Most people with peace of mind sleep through the night with only an

1

occasional muttering. Dead people are very quiet. And so are many students attempting to give their first speech before a group. Their hands tremble, mental functions cease, and vocal cords constrict until their first utterance is only a pitiful bleat.

Why is this? They are scared, of course. It's stage fright—the affliction that has devastated everyone from the beginning speech student to the incomparable actor, Sir Laurence Olivier.

The fear stems not from the threat of being shot dead in one's tracks for a bobbled word; rather, it is the fear of making a mistake and looking foolish. Speech class can help you overcome fears related to speaking in public. It will help you organize your thoughts so they may be expressed smoothly. It will give you confidence—a valuable attribute in today's fast-moving and sometimes overpowering world.

Why is confidence important? Consider the following true story and perhaps you will understand what can happen when confidence is either undeveloped or destroyed.

Sure beats making a speech.

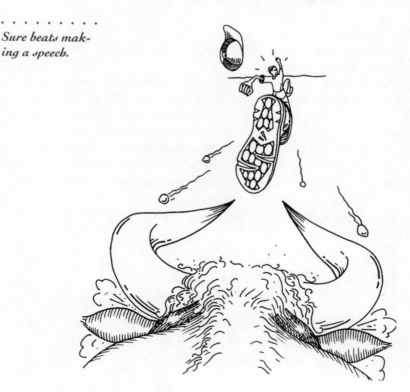

When a gentleman we know was a teenager, he transferred to a new school. One morning, about three days after he had started classes, the principal informed him that she was going to call on him to give a short talk during an assembly. She briefly told him the topic he was to speak on and then swept down the hall before the shy youth could learn further details.

Terrified, he attended the assembly and, sure enough, was called upon to stand and speak to a group of several hundred. His mind was blank with fear—a fear more intense than the time he was cornered by a large, very angry bull. He escaped the bull, but he did not escape the consequences of his unintelligible babble that day in the assembly.

He did not have the confidence to open his mouth again for nearly 30 years. He gave much thought to ways of avoiding occasions when he might be called upon to speak. He had one sentence to recite in the high school play, but was "ill" and unable to be there the night of the performance.

In later years, he attended occasional service club meetings, such as the Jaycees, but never joined. Whenever he had to introduce himself to such a group, he would have to write down his name and place of employment so he wouldn't forget.

The point of this dismal story is that to be able to speak with relative comfort in a public situation, a person must have confidence. Confidence is acquired in two primary ways—knowledge and practice. Speech class will help you develop confidence by giving you knowledge and opportunities to practice.

The speaker's responsibility is not only to communicate ideas in a speech, but also to convey to the audience members that he truly desires them to absorb these ideas.

Until you get to this point, you may feel like giving a speech in private to a friend, or to yourself. But once you hear your classmates speaking in class, you'll conclude that you can do as well as they do and will give it a try. This course is designed to get you to the point where you will enjoy sharing ideas with others.

Speech instructors seldom find a real silver tongue among their beginning students. More often, the typical student is shy and feels awkward. You are not expected to be a great or even minimally acceptable speaker when you begin a basic speech class. You are not there because you *know* how to speak; you are there to *learn* how to speak. Speech class is the place to make mistakes. Other students will understand, and the instructor will be delighted because he or she can start helping you over rough spots. Make your mistakes in class and you won't make nearly as many when it counts—when you are out in the world.

A benefit of mistakes is that you may learn from them, both your own and the mistakes of others. Learning what not to do is often as important as learning what to do.

☞ Summary

In every class there will be a few hardy souls who enjoy getting up to share their ideas with an audience. We applaud you and acknowledge that the class will benefit from your positive attitude. At the same time, we know the majority of you will find stage fright to be a major problem.

Take comfort in the fact that you are not the only one who is worried and that your instructor understands that time, patience, and practice will gradually bring you to the point where you are willing, with preparation, to stand before the class and do the best that you can. Chances are you will do well, and the audience, knowing you are willing to do your best for them, will appreciate your effort enough to listen attentively.

☞ Skill Builders

1. The First Speech

Before we discuss the more formal aspects of giving a speech, let's try a simple activity to help us get our feet wet.

1

While remaining in your seat, tell the class the things about yourself that you feel are important, not what you think the audience wants to hear. Remember, in all speeches, the only criteria are what the speaker feels to be most important.

This is an impromptu speech, and no preparation is necessary. After all, you already know about yourself.

Listed below are a few things you might choose to tell your audience.

- Name (always a good way to start).

- Home town, places you have lived, and so forth.

- Family information:

  Parents' occupations.

  Brothers and sisters.

  Family pets, favorite car.

- Course of study and future job plans.

- Past and present jobs.

- Memorable vacations (good or bad, but memorable).

- Favorite/least favorite people.

- Important friendships (buddies or romantic).

- Future expectations beyond a job:

  Type of home you would like to live in.

  Hobbies you would like to develop.

  A special place you someday want to visit.

These speeches can be *no longer* than two minutes. "How can I possibly talk about all of this in two minutes?" you may ask.

The point is, you can't. And this is true for all speeches that you will give. You will always know much more about any topic you select than you will have time to share with your audience. Learn to choose the most important parts.

So, with no preparation, in two minutes, state your name and give as much information as you can without speaking too fast. Do not worry if the speech is shorter than two minutes. Even in a small amount of time, the class will learn enough about you to

1

begin to get to know you; class members will enjoy hearing about you.

A caution on nervousness: If, after you state your name, your mind goes blank, simply look at your instructor and say, "Help!" The instructor, with a question or topic, will help you to get going again.

The listeners in this series of speeches will not be taking notes, nor will they comment on the speeches. But listen closely to others so you will get to know them, and listen for ideas they may give you for your own talk.

2. Get Comfortable with Conferences

Your instructor is a very important part of your support system in this class. The better your instructor knows you, the more individual attention you can get.

After the above speech, if you feel the instructor could use more specialized information about you, make an appointment for a one-on-one conference.

This conference will be a good time to voice your fears about giving a speech, or even to tell your instructor that the class appears it will be more positive than you thought. Instructors like this kind of information—it helps them do a better job.

Two

[SPEECH BASICS]

By studying this chapter, you will:

- Learn how to choose a topic that is right for you.

- Learn where to find sources of material for a speech.

- Learn to be flexible when making a presentation.

- Learn the value of proper physical appearance for your speech.

*O*ne of the problems with a speech class is that it is called "speech class" and you are expected to give "speeches." Semantically speaking, this may be a mistake. The word speech can conjure up visions of a sophisticated lecturer standing on a stage, giving a masterful presentation to thousands of awe-struck listeners.

· ·

[TALK; DON'T SPEAK]

Would it make you more comfortable if the instructor said you are assigned to give a "talk"? Talking is easy; making a speech is scary. In a basic speech class, all you will be doing is talking to your classmates, not addressing the United Nations.

One of the brightest people we know, a woman who has risen to the highest levels of authority in one of the nation's leading private colleges, is an expert at addressing audiences. At a moment's notice, she can expound on any number of topics and do it very well indeed.

Years ago, she was frequently asked to make such presentations and cheerfully did so, but only for those persons who asked her to give a "talk." If anyone made the mistake of asking her to give a "speech," her face turned white, she trembled, and chances were she would decline the invitation.

She loved to talk and did it well, but she was convinced that she could not give a speech.

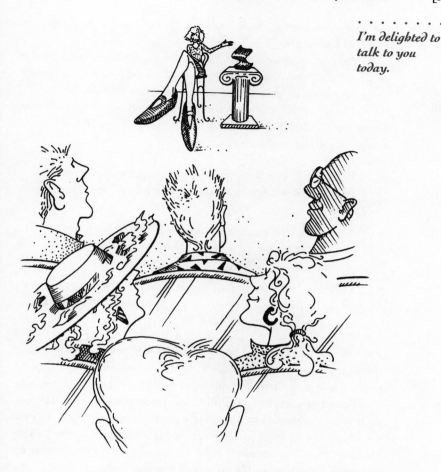

I'm delighted to talk to you today.

So, as a first step toward building confidence, let's stop "speechifying" and start "talking." Because that is what you will be doing for the present. The United Nations can come later.

[BE PREPARED]

The time is here for you to begin *preparing* for your first talk before your class. The talk may simply be taking part in a group discussion or it may be a slightly more formal exercise wherein

2

you stand before the class. Either way, knowing your subject is much of the battle.

As you discovered in your autobiography speech in the previous chapter, you can already speak easily on a great many topics concerning you, your family, and your friends.

Many of your topics for speeches come from personal experiences. But you also have other areas of interest that you would enjoy sharing with the class.

- Everybody needs to know about car care. If you have special knowledge in this area, it is perfect speech material.

- Have you had experience with animals? Share funny incidents you have had with them, or tell how to care for them.

- One easy way to find a topic is to listen to other speeches in class. Almost assuredly, something that someone else says will give you an idea.

When you are compiling material for a class presentation, spend the time it takes to do it right. Use an ample number of sources and pick through your information to find which aspects are of most interest to you. Build your presentation around these. If you don't immediately understand something, study it until you do. Don't try to bluff in a speech (or talk). If you know you're bluffing, your confidence will be damaged. One of the secrets to knowing your material is to select a topic with which you are already acquainted. Talk about things you have done, things that interest you.

[NOTECARDS: PROS AND CONS]

Some people like to use notecards to jot down the outline of their speech or presentation. You can put one topic on each note card, or you can write a topic and a few facts or items of note to spur you on to making your point. Notecards can remind you of the most important things you want to say—they can help keep you on track and make sure you don't walk away feeling that there was just one more point you wanted to make.

Notecards can also help reduce anxiety. Even if you don't refer to your notecards during a presentation, you'll have a safe feeling knowing that they are there *if you need them*. And the simple act of outlining your speech or presentation on notecards will help you organize your speech in your mind and act as one last reinforcer that you are ready and prepared to speak.

But using notecards also has its drawbacks. There are a number of reasons for this. One reason not to use notecards is that some people rely on them *too* much. If you read directly from your cards, rather than use the cards to stimulate your thoughts, the cards can become a crutch that causes more tension than it provides security.

For some speakers, notecards get in the way of a creative flow of ideas. You may have a brilliant idea right in the middle of your speech, but if you feel tied to the order of material outlined on your cards, you may feel uneasy about expressing your great idea.

Experiment with notecards to see if using them reduces or creates anxiety. Their effect will, of course, vary from person to person. Above all, make sure your creativity is given free rein. After all, you are the one sharing your skills and insights with the audience — they want to listen to *you*.

[MEMORIZE?]

If you don't use notes, maybe you should memorize your talk. Right? Wrong! For sure, memorization is going to make your speech sound rigid. You have heard speakers who have memorized the whole thing — they drone on and on in a smothering monotone. Not for long will the members of the audience subject themselves to such abuse. They stop listening.

In order to keep an audience attentive, the speaker needs to present material in a fresh, bright, conversational tone. This is not always easy; even experienced speakers have difficulty.

Although it is bad enough to be boring, it is infinitely worse to forget a word or phrase in a memorized speech. If you do, the

2

whole thing will probably go out the window. You can remember nothing else. Your brain becomes oatmeal. You are dead. But if you have chosen a topic you know well, you can rattle on and take a responsive audience with you.

There is another instance when notecards come in handy. Sometimes you will need to write down some material that would be nearly impossible to store in your memory. This could be numbers, lists of statistics, or any sort of complicated data. However, it is not always sufficient merely to read this material to an audience. Perhaps it should be written on a chalkboard or presented as some other type of visual aid.

[LOOK THE PART]

Another way to build confidence is to look sharp and feel sharp the day you are to speak. Don't go schlepping into class in decrepit thongs and decaying blue jeans.

A speech instructor we know is fond of recalling one of her favorite students and likes to tell of the often extreme effort he devoted to speech class. "George was the typical country kid going to college in the big city. He loved it and tried to do everything right, especially in speech class.

"One day, after hearing advice on the benefits of looking nice for a speech, he came to class wearing a new suit. I could tell it was new because the price tag was still on the sleeve.

"After class I asked him, 'George, why do you have the price tag still on your suit?'

"He looked at me like I was very stupid and said, 'Because that shows this is a new suit—otherwise, nobody would know.'"

Have a good night's sleep, and spiff yourself up. Eat a decent breakfast. Go to the bathroom before class. Smile—this is going to be fun. You are a star!

[ANALYZING YOUR AUDIENCE]

2

Tailoring the language of your presentation to your audience is another consideration in giving speeches. Don't use words the average member of your audience won't understand. Conversely, if you are speaking to an audience whose members are more highly educated, it won't hurt to use some "big" words. The advantage of using big words is that they often allow the speaker to express ideas more exactly.

Of course I left the tag on. It's new.

2

Slang can be touchy. Using teenage slang when addressing an older group can confuse some listeners. If you are facing an audience of people unfamiliar with the English language and totally unfamiliar with its slang, you must speak very carefully or run the risk of misunderstandings or mixed messages.

[PRACTICE, PRACTICE, PRACTICE]

After you have gathered and organized the material you need (we'll tell you how in a later chapter), the next step is to practice your presentation two or three times. Deliver your talk in front of a mirror, if you don't feel too foolish doing so, or practice before family and friends. A word of caution should you plan to practice with a tape recorder: If you have not heard your recorded voice before, be prepared for a shock; you will probably think you sound horrible. As a beginning speech student, using a recorder (audio or video) and worrying about how you look and sound will distract you.

Practice as often as you can in a class. The more often you speak, the easier it becomes. In fact, there is a danger of becoming too enamored with speaking . . . witness the endless droning of some politicians.

☞ *Summary*

Stage fright can be controlled by learning speech basics. By concentrating on talking rather than speaking, you can teach yourself to become comfortable when speaking in front of a group.

Take the time to familiarize yourself with speech preparation, begin to think about choosing speech topics and speech aids, and analyze your general appearance as a speaker.

Above all, get ready to practice, practice, practice!

Skill Builders

1. Topics for all!

* Write 10 topics (using full sentences) for impromptu speeches that anybody can give.

* Give these to the instructor, who will judge their acceptability. If you don't get 10 good topics immediately, keep writing until the instructor says you do.

* For the rest of the course, as time allows, draw these topics out of a box and give one-minute speeches on them.

After you give this one-minute talk, select the next person to draw. Students who have spoken may not speak again until all have had turns.

Three

[PLATFORM MANNER AND DELIVERY]

By studying this chapter, you will:

- **Learn that the performance of a speech begins as you stand to approach the platform and ends only when you return to your seat.**

- **Develop a platform manner.**

- **Learn the purpose of eye contact.**

A speech does not begin with the speaker's first word. It begins when you leave your seat and begin to walk to the podium. If you walk as if you're marching to the gallows (and many do), nobody is going to want to hear what you have to say. Walk tall. Show confidence, even if you don't feel it. This chapter will give you the tools to build and maintain speaking confidence.

3

[FIVE STEPS FOR SUCCESS]

➤ PAUSE AND RELAX

Upon reaching the podium, pause 5 or 10 seconds. During this time, look around the room, establish eye contact, and wait for the audience to quiet down. At least this is how it will appear. What you are *really* doing is trying to recover from the shock of looking over an audience, trying to get your Adam's apple back where it belongs. The pause is your opportunity to quiet your galloping heart and reclaim your brain from the quagmire of panic.

The audience, of course, cannot read your mind. To them, your pause shows that you have grace and dignity, and you intend to speak only when you have their undivided attention. After about 10 seconds, you should be calm and ready to begin.

➤ TO GESTURE OR NOT TO GESTURE

As a rule of thumb, any action or mannerism that calls attention to itself is bad. It is said that former President Richard Nixon would practice his gestures right along with his speech, instead of letting the gestures come naturally. When he made his presentation, people knew there was something unnatural about it; they were often distracted when Nixon made a studied gesture but made it a split second too late to match his words.

The podium as a gallows.

3

Speech class will let you try various platform manners— standing, pacing, gesturing, and so on. Experiment until you determine which style is best for you.

➤ THE QUESTION OF EYE CONTACT

No matter how you stand or pace, you must maintain eye contact with the audience. If you are not looking at them, you are saying, "I don't want you here, I don't want you to listen." The audience feels this, and its members don't listen. And if the audience is not listening, why are you speaking?

*Look at their
noses.*

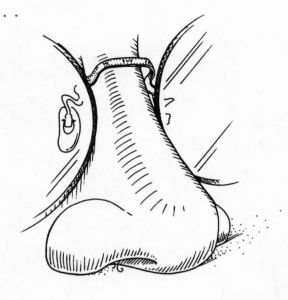

Some speakers are uncomfortable maintaining direct eye contact with members of the audience. If you find this is true for you, look at their noses instead. No one will ever know the difference.

➤ DEVELOP YOUR OWN STYLE

There are few rules on how a speaker should act once the actual presentation begins. Should you stand, sit, or pace back and forth during a speech? Who knows? Each speaker is unique; each speaker has a unique style. What might be most effective for one person would be a disaster for another. And situations, too, can influence platform manner. If you are speaking to the Ladies Aid on the poetry of Emily Dickinson, it might be appropriate to remain behind or near the podium. If you are advocating a strike to your union local, you can probably pace or even run all over the room if you are so moved. Adopt a style that is most comfortable for you and meets the needs of the audience.

➤ WALK; DON'T RUN

When you have finished your talk, there will be an inclination to dash back to the safety of your chair. This would immediately tell the audience, "I did a terrible job. I feel so stupid!"

Before you make this unwise move, realize there is a strong possibility that the audience is thinking you did a fine job. But if you flee the platform in this negative manner, the audience may agree with your self-assessment.

Here is what to do: After your last word, pause, briefly establish eye contact with everybody in the audience, and return to your seat with dignity. You have done your best.

A point on dignity: Many speakers end their presentations with a modest "thank you," supposedly thanking the audience for its attention. This is the reverse of what it should be. If you have shared your special ideas with the audience, the audience owes you thanks. A thank you to the audience almost seems an apology. Don't do it.

You've mastered the five steps and feel pretty good. But what if you just can't conquer your own fears? Well, think of the worst thing that could happen. As Sophia, one of the characters on the television series *The Golden Girls*, used to say, "Picture this."

The worst case

The student's worst fears are realized. His name is called and he must speak before the class.

Trembling, he trudges, head down, to the lectern and seizes it in a death grip. Usually, it is one of those little lecterns that stands on top of a table or desk. The knuckles of his hands grow white from lack of circulation; so do the "knuckles" of his mind.

As the tension in his hands and brain increases, one leg will wrap itself around the other and he must grip the lectern ever harder to keep from falling over. Then he starts to sweat from all this physical and mental exertion.

As he stands there, looking blankly at the lectern, something in the far corner of his brain says, "You had better start talking."

So, without warning, his head jerks up and, eyes wild, he fires off a machine-gun burst of unintelligible words. Of course, he scares himself by this outburst and forgets what he is doing. In a worst-case scenario, he repeats the same dismal performance, this time accompanying himself with the squeaking of the lectern as he slides it around the desk. He doesn't hear that, of course, but the audience is aghast.

While he is creating his own personal hell at the lectern, he is terrifying those scheduled to speak next and no doubt, because of his influence, their presentations will be nearly as miserable. You want to talk about empathy? Here is empathy at its worst. It is a nightmare for everybody.

At this point the speaker has no possibility of accomplishing anything he had planned. He can't even remember the topic. The aching legs and clutching hands have strangled his thought processes—words come randomly from his mouth.

Finally, the best thing that could happen, happens. No, he doesn't drop dead, but it occurs to him he might just as well stop. So he bolts back to his seat, sliding into it like a baseball player slides into home plate.

The speaker is happy just to be alive. But the audience has been plunged into a pit of depression. You can see a black cloud in the classroom.

[HOW TO AVOID DISASTER]

How could the would-be speaker avoid this disgrace?
Proper platform manner would help. Proper platform manner sometimes requires some acting, and you will find that if you act

convincingly enough, you will even convince yourself. You will become what you pretend to be.

1.   When your name is called, force a pleasant look on your face. Think, "I am prepared, I am ready." Stand up, throw your shoulders back, and stride purposefully to the lectern.

2.   When you get there, place your palms flat on the lectern. This avoids physical tensions in your arms and hands.

3.   To begin, place your feet comfortably apart and flat on the floor. Keep your knees slightly flexed to avoid tension in your legs.

4.   Look at the audience — all of them. Take time to look around; make sure they are ready to listen.

This pause will seems like a long one to you, but audiences always want you to be ready, and they will be patient. This will provide you with positive empathy — they want you to succeed because your success will contribute to their own success when it is their turn. Remember, you are all in this together, you are not alone.

During the pause, you may become aware that your speech material is ready to come out of your mouth on the prompting of one part of your brain, while another part of your brain sits apart, praying for your success. It is normal for beginning speakers to have this dual thought process. As you become more experienced, the parts of your brain will rejoin, to your benefit. Don't force it; it just happens.

As you learn to relax, you will find gestures will come naturally. Do not plan gestures in advance. They will come on their own as you develop your platform manner.

➤ FILL IN THE BLANKS

What if your mind goes blank in middle of a speech? What will you do? Turn to the instructor or the class and say, "My mind just went blank. What was I saying?"

This happens in everyday conversations — so why not here? Ask for a memory jog. You will get it, and you are on your way again.

3

Burl Ives knows the secret

The greatest American balladeer of all time is Burl Ives. Mr. Ives performed for much of the 20th century and was still making appearances when he was well into his 80s.

His voice was as pure as ever but time had taken a toll and in his later years he became forgetful. Sometimes, songs he had been singing for more than half a century would escape him.

He would warn his audiences in advance and asked them to bear with him.

Sure enough. During a performance attended by the author, Mr. Ives indeed did forget. But his songs were so familiar that the helpful audience sang the missing words to him until Mr. Ives got back on the track. The audience loved it, and think how gratified Mr. Ives must have been that people regarded him and his life's work with such affection.

☞ Summary

Just getting up on stage and delivering a speech can, of course, be terrifying. Sure, you realize that a big part of overcoming your fears is being aware of them, but learning some concrete facts about the mechanics of delivery can go a long way toward building confidence.

Get a handle on the five steps to success, and you'll be on your way to effective speaking. Focus on relaxing, learning about gestures, making eye contact, developing your own style, and exiting the podium gracefully.

Skill Builders

1.   Stand and Deliver

Deliver a series of impromptu speeches (draw from your topics in the last Skill Builders). Use this opportunity to walk to the podium, deliver a short speech, and then walk back to your seat. Maintain eye contact throughout.

Your instructor and classmates should make suggestions for improvement. Example: "Instead of standing on one foot, stand on two; take a step once in a while."

Or, "Don't clutch the podium so hard that your knuckles turn white. Lay your palms flat on it—maybe some gestures will show up."

These comments will serve as models for the types of comments the class will soon be making in discussion of formal speeches.

Four

[DISCUSSING SPEECHES]

By studying this chapter, you will:

- **Learn to initiate a speech.**

- **Master constructive criticism.**

- **Gracefully accept class comments about your speech.**

In many speech classes, it is customary for students to discuss and critique speeches given by class members. This discussion usually revolves around three points—how the speaker looks, how the speaker sounds, and what the speaker says. If the audience doesn't notice how a speaker looks or sounds, but only notices the speaker's message, the speaker has done a good job. Remember, anything that calls attention to itself is bad. After all, the aim of the speaker is not to impress (or distract) the audience with his or her platform manner; the aim is to get them to listen to what he or she has to say. Learning about constructive criticism now will prepare you to comment on your classmates' formal speeches (Chapters 5–8).

4

[CONSTRUCTIVE CRITICISM]

When you critique a speech you should mention both the good and bad points of the presentation. Comments on the bad points should be in the form of constructive suggestions.

Classes are often conducted so that students start speaking and critiquing at the same time. In the first few speeches, comments should deal only with the positive aspects. Here are examples of positive comments:

- The speaker approached the lectern with an air of confidence.

- He established good eye contact before starting to talk.

- His presentation was free of distracting mannerisms.

- Her voice could be heard easily.

- The information was interesting.

- The material was presented in a logical way.

- The topic reminded me of something that happened to me.

For the first speech, leave to the instructor the dirty work of telling the speaker what is wrong. The instructor will be experienced enough to follow each speech with constructive suggestions for improvement.

There is a certain etiquette to observe when listening to or critiquing the speech of a classmate. An unguarded snicker from the audience can destroy a novice speaker. When the time comes that you are asked to offer suggestions for improvement, be kind. Don't wreck someone's potential to be a good speaker.

There is another reason for the critic in a basic speech class to avoid rudeness. If you give a fellow student a bad time, that student or the student's friends are going to skewer you when your time at the podium arrives. It may take weeks, but sooner or later you will get yours. And deservedly so.

➤ ACCEPTING CRITICISM

Getting feedback for a speech can be painful for a beginning speaker. It is great to hear all of the nice things your fellow students say about your effort. But even positively constructed criticism can sometimes be hurtful if you let it. Do not let criticism discourage you, any more than you should let the favorable comments swell your ego.

A suggestion for improvement is one of many ways that your classmates are trying to support you in speech class, and they are going to be as kind as possible to you because they want you to be kind to them.

If somebody really does a nasty job of criticizing you, though, console yourself with the fact that sooner or later you are going to get a shot at your critic. What goes around comes around. Or, to put it biblically, "As ye sow, so shall ye reap."

[INTERACTION]

Discussion of speeches benefits everybody. Audience members, too, can learn a great deal about what to do and what not to do when they make their own presentations.

➤ PROMOTE YOUR SKILLS, NOT YOURSELF

Further, and perhaps most importantly, class members will learn how to function in a discussion situation. When you are at work, you will frequently be involved in group discussions with employers and other employees. If you can conduct yourself well in such discussions, the path to future promotion grows wider. Employers are impressed with those who can express their ideas clearly. They are not impressed with the lumpish employee who cowers silently at the end of the table.

But be careful—employers are irritated by persons who belabor the group with streams of blather. Speech class discussions will give you an idea of when you should be talking and, just as importantly, when you should be listening.

When the time arrives for students to begin offering suggestions for improvement, there are numerous things to bear in mind. Perhaps most importantly, the critic should mix the good and the bad, giving the good far more emphasis. No matter how terrible the presentation you have just witnessed, there is something good to be said, if only, "You sure don't sweat much for a nervous person." (That's a joke. Don't you dare say it.)

Although it's advisable to focus attention on the speaker's strengths, you shouldn't feel compelled to *always* say good things about everybody. Before long, nonstop praise will ring hollow and unbelievable.

However, a number of members of a class may make the same good comments. This is OK—hearing such comments from a lot of people has more credence than hearing several good comments from only one person. This, though, only applies to the good. Once a criticism is made, others in the class should not belabor the point. Don't worry. The person on the receiving end will remember.

[DON'T RUSH!]

A common mistake made by speakers is to start their presentations too quickly, without a pause to get ready. This often causes the speaker to become off balance both mentally and physically and have a hard time catching up.

How should the critic approach this situation? Not this way: "You started off so fast that the whole speech sounded bad."

Don't tell what you don't like unless you can offer a remedy. Half-baked criticism doesn't help anybody. How about this for a more humane and effective approach: "Perhaps you would be more comfortable at the beginning of your speech if you paused a little longer. Then you could get yourself settled and start the first sentence a little more slowly."

Or this: "I really enjoyed the approach you used to begin your speech, but I wish that you had started more slowly so that I would have had time to absorb it."

. . . .

Summary

When it comes to criticism in a speech class, the Golden Rule assumes particular importance. "Do unto others what you would have done unto you" certainly applies when you know that the classmate you critique today will be the classmate who critiques you tomorrow.

Keep in mind that the best criticism is constructive—it should help the speaker identify strengths and analyze weaknesses. The purpose of in-class criticism is to share ideas and insights, *not* to embarrass the speaker.

Skill Builder

1.   Focus on the Positive

The three basic areas to be considered in critiquing a speech are how the speaker looks (his physical appearance and platform manner), how the speaker sounds (enunciation, volume, and so on), and what the person says (content and organization).

Under each of these three basic areas, write a list of four imagined positive comments and a list of four constructive criticisms, positively worded.

For example:

- "The speaker had eye contact with every member of the audience."

- "The speaker had good eye contact for those in the middle section of the audience. For the next speech, she should try to include eye contact for everyone."

- "I liked the way the speaker spoke so clearly — I could hear everything from the back of the room."

- "The speaker's topic — the Gulf War — was quite interesting. It could have been even more powerful if he had moved the section on possible causes toward the beginning of the speech rather than saving it until the end."

2. **Monitor Your Progress**

Use the critique form on the next page as you evaluate your own and your classmates' speeches over the length of the course. If you feel uncomfortable critiquing a classmate out loud, the form could help you present constructive criticism in a less personal way.

PROGRESS ASSESSMENT FORM

Speaker: Topic: Overall Rating:

	Needs Improvement			Excellent	
Appearance:					
Dressed appropriately	1	2	3	4	5
Self-confident	1	2	3	4	5
Doesn't show nervousness	1	2	3	4	5
Makes eye contact	1	2	3	4	5
Delivery:					
Appropriate voice volume	1	2	3	4	5
Clear pronunciation	1	2	3	4	5
Effective shifts in tone	1	2	3	4	5
Appropriate gestures	1	2	3	4	5
Emotion and humor	1	2	3	4	5
Content:					
Interesting topic	1	2	3	4	5
Logical organization	1	2	3	4	5
Effective persuasion	1	2	3	4	5
Informative	1	2	3	4	5
Relevance to audience	1	2	3	4	5

4

Five

THE ONE-POINT SPEECH

By studying this chapter, you will:

- Deliver a formal (but abbreviated) speech in front of an audience.

- Experience class members' reactions to your speech.

1

2

3

4

5

6

7

8

9

Your first speech in front of the class will be a one-point speech (or talk).

This speech will contain a single, simple idea that should not take more than two or three minutes to present. There are numerous reasons for the use of the one-point speech:

1. *To experience, perhaps for the first time, getting up in front of an audience.*

2. *To hear your own voice for the first time in a classroom situation.*

3. *To notice what physical posture makes you comfortable or uncomfortable and thus begin to develop your own personal platform manner.*

4. *To choose an idea suitable for the first speech.*

5. *To pick out a positive quality from each of the speeches presented.*

6. *To observe what works and what does not work in speeches by others.*

7. *To demonstrate appropriate behavior on approaching and leaving the podium and in beginning and ending the speech.*

8. *To use proper eye contact with the audience during the speech.*

[CHOOSING A TOPIC]

Logically, if you are going to make a presentation, you should probably have something to present. In other words, it is time to choose a topic. Very often, this is the most difficult part of the assignment.

When you receive your assignment from your instructor, make certain you understand it. Don't immediately start racking your brain for a topic. Instead, tuck what information you have in

Inspiration

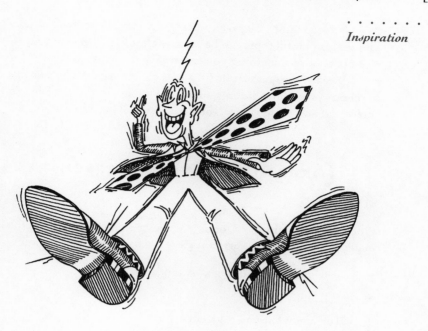

the back of your mind and just let it rattle around in there for a couple of days. Then, out of the clear blue, the idea may hit; you will have your topic, and you can proceed from there. Trust your subconscious—it will take care of you.

But suppose it doesn't? Suppose there is no bolt of inspiration? Now what will you do? Perhaps a little advice from your instructor will be helpful, or ask friends and relatives for suggestions. Even if these suggestions are not exactly right, tuck them in the back of your mind and let them rest. A topic will come.

➤ YOU'RE THE EXPERT

One consideration in choosing a topic is to find an area in which you are the expert, where nobody knows more than you do. Obviously, then, you should be thinking of talking about yourself or your family, about your worst experience or your best experience, or about your pets, or your children.

Select a topic that gives you pleasure to talk or think about, although a painful topic can be equally effective. Whichever way you go, choose something you can treat enthusiastically.

It really doesn't matter (in a one-point speech) whether the audience is initially interested in the topic. If the speaker is interested and enthusiastic, the audience will be also.

[ORGANIZING YOUR SPEECH]

Once you have chosen a topic, your next step is to organize the material. An old army sergeant gave the following instruction:

- Tell 'em what you're gonna tell 'em.

- Tell 'em.

- Tell 'em what you told 'em.

The one-point speech can be divided into three types: explanation, illustration, and comparison.

➤ EXPLANATION

The explanation speech tells the audience the "why" of something—it "explains." Let's take the "army" method, apply it to an instance of explanation, and see how such a one-point speech could be presented.

The one-point speech, for purposes of a speech class, should begin, "I would like to tell you . . . ." For example, "I would like to tell you about the thing I hated most about my job last summer." Note that this opening statement is very specific—the speaker is not going to tell about the whole job, or several things she disliked about it. She is going to cover only one topic—the *worst* part of the job. Note that this opening sentence conforms with the "army" method: "Tell 'em what you're gonna tell 'em."

Next, the speaker "tells 'em." "The worst part of my job, which was working construction, was the preparation we would have to make before we took our lunch break. We had to kill all the rattlesnakes that crept into the shade of the lunch area."

The worst part of my job last summer...

5

At this point, the speaker may elaborate briefly on the single idea. "Sometimes lunch breaks were pretty short — we were given a half hour and it often took 20 minutes to kill the snakes."

Again, for the purposes of a class exercise, the speaker closes by telling the audience what he or she told them. A typical ending to the speech would be, "Today, I have told you the worst part of my job last summer."

➤ ILLUSTRATION

Illustration means telling a story to make a point, perhaps the best type of material one can use in a speech. How did Christ so effectively reach his listeners? He told parables, or stories. Who can forget the story of the Prodigal Son and its application to life, both temporal and spiritual? How about the famous fables of Aesop—the terms *sour grapes* and *dog in the manger* have become parts of our language.

As an example of how an illustrative story can be used, let's pretend the speaker is trying to give his audience some insight into one aspect of the character of Sir Winston Churchill, the acid-tongued prime minister of England:

> It is no secret that Sir Winston had a fondness for the bottle and at times would slip more deeply into his cups than many thought prudent. Then, woe betide the unwary person who would venture a critical remark toward the irascible old man. One time at a party, Sir Winston had been overindulging when he encountered a dragonlike dowager, glutted with self-importance and driven by a compulsion to criticize her fellow man.
>
> "Sir Winston," she sniffed, radiating disgust, "you are drunk!"
>
> "Yes, Madam," he replied. "And you are ugly. But in the morning I will be sober and you will still be ugly."

➤ COMPARISON

A speaker will often explain an unfamiliar subject to an audience by comparing that subject to one with which the audience is familiar. Comparisons are useful in many situations for making one's ideas understandable. There are comparisons everywhere:

- How big? About the size of a bread box.

- How small? No bigger than a minute.

- How ugly? Uglier than homemade sin.

- How mean? Meaner than a snake.

- How cold? As cold as the day my brass monkey was frostbitten.

In normal conversation, explanations, illustrations, and comparisons, seemingly thrown together with wild abandon, in fact are used singly and in combination only where appropriate. Use your instincts—say what you have to say out loud to a friend. If it sounds like good conversation, you probably have the right components in the right places.

*But you, Madam,
will still be ugly.*

5

➤ TELL THE WORLD!

Once you have decided what your one-point speech is to be, practice it out loud, either by yourself or to a friend. It is important for your idea to go from your brain to your mouth so that you are not surprised by the results during your actual presentation. Do not write your speech; do not memorize it. Just a few out-loud practices will prepare you for this first formal speaking exercise.

☞   ## Summary

The key to the one-point speech is to be brief. We will say it again:

- Tell 'em what you're gonna tell 'em.
- Tell 'em (using explanation, illustration, or comparison).
- Tell 'em what you told 'em.

☞   ## Skill Builders

1. Putting it Together

Based on the information in this chapter, be prepared to develop and deliver a one-point speech to your class. This speech can explain, illustrate, or compare.

Break up into small groups and choose one person at a time to deliver his or her speech to the group. Critique the speeches within the group.

2. Go Public!

Each person should deliver his or her very brief speech to the class as a whole (time permitting). Be prepared to draw on your knowledge of platform delivery, and be ready to field and offer constructive criticism. Above all, have FUN!

5

Six

[THE INFORMATIVE SPEECH]

By studying this chapter, you will:

- Learn the mechanics of the motivated sequence, a vital component of all speeches.

- Be able to correctly construct a need/proposition sentence.

- Learn to think of this speech as a chain of one-point speeches.

The informative speech is not calculated to move mountains or change the world. It only gives information — the speaker is going to tell how to do something or relay other knowledge.

For the informative speech, you'll take everything you learned in the one-point speech and then construct a chain of one-point speeches. The chain must be constructed so your audience will become interested and stay interested enough to keep listening.

[THE BUILDING BLOCKS]

Informative speeches are very simple to construct, although your initial feeling is that it might be more difficult. Do not be misled or intimidated — it's really an easy process.

Just as the informative speech is built on a chain of one-point speeches, the types of material in the informative speech will be used to construct the persuasive speech. (You will learn this in Chapter 8.) If you learn the construction of the informative speech and use the correct terminology, you will find it easy to progress to the next step. If you do not learn the steps of building an informative speech, your chances for successful progression are slim. You can see that there is a great deal more to successful speaking than merely talking!

[THE MOTIVATED SEQUENCE: STEPS TO BUILDING AN INFORMATIVE SPEECH]

In order to move your audience to listen, you need to develop fluency in a type of organization called the "motivated sequence." This organization was originally developed by a group of speech instructors and psychologists to follow the way most normal people think. If you speak in a way that matches the audience's thought patterns, it will be easier for the audience to follow you.

6

The components of the motivated sequence as used in the **informative** speech are:

- Attention step.
- Need-proposition step.
- Satisfaction step.
- Conclusion step.

The motivated sequence will vary somewhat in other types of speeches as you'll see when you learn the steps for each type of speech.

➤ ATTENTION STEP

To give a speech successfully, it is necessary to have your audience listening to you. From the outset, you must grasp their attention — pull them away from their thoughts and make them listen to you. If you cannot accomplish this — if your attention step is not powerful — your speech will not succeed.

There are seven kinds of legitimate attention-getting approaches that we are about to explore. But before getting into these, it might be instructive to recall a story told by a friend.

6

When the friend was a child, he attended a state fair and, while wandering around the fairgrounds, came upon a seedy-looking gentleman setting up some sound equipment on the tailgate of a truck. The boy watched this operation for a short time and was walking away when the seedy-looking gentleman spoke into a microphone. "Okay, Joe. Bring over the big snakes."

The boy heard this and wasn't about to leave if there were some big snakes to be seen. Other people must have felt the same way, because soon a sizable crowd began to gather. The seedy-looking gentleman continued setting up his tailgate, occasionally advising an unseen "Joe" to get the snakes ready.

The man on the tailgate was a pitchman and was selling some kind of tonic—just like the traveling medicine shows of the Old West.

Suddenly, the pitchman straightened from his work and launched into the sales pitch for his tonic. Nobody cared about that at first, but they waited around to see the snakes. Of course, there never were any snakes, and of course the pitchman sold a surprising number of bottles of his tonic.

Certainly not a legitimate approach to use with an audience, but sometimes you do what you have to do.

It has been determined by some psychologists and speech instructors that an attention step needs to be a minimum of two minutes in length to be effective. No matter how long the remainder of the speech will be, the attention step should probably be at least two minutes. It takes at least that long to draw each listener out of his own thoughts and make him want to mentally accompany the speaker.

➤ SEVEN APPROACHES FOR GETTING ATTENTION

When the time comes to make a speech, here are the seven approaches that are effective to use for an attention step. Use one or more of them to help you assemble two minutes of good, strong material.

1.   **Reference to the subject.** The speaker simply starts talking about the subject or something closely related to it. She hopes to draw the attention of the audience by using material in which she knows the audience is interested. For example, let's suppose a speaker is to address a convention of child psychologists on the topic of childhood development. Her opening remarks might be about inventor Thomas Edison and how apparently he was a slow learner as a child.

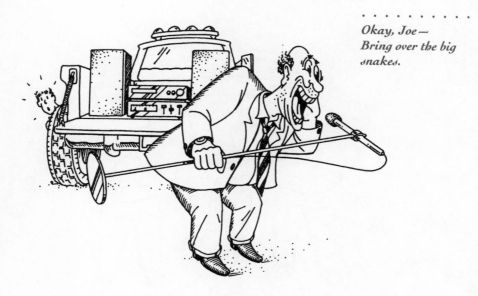

Okay, Joe—Bring over the big snakes.

Perhaps the speech is to deal with the importance of advertising. The speaker could open by giving examples of billboards he has recently seen, or the alluring and provocative aspects of well-known television commercials. By the time the audience has heard these topics, it will have a good idea of the speech topic.

2.   **Reference to the occasion.** This is the one you hear all the time — "I'm so glad to see so many of you here at the church budget meeting tonight." This is a good, solid opening line and works well in situations where the audience's attendance is voluntary.

It probably would not work well, though, were you to say, "I'm so glad to see all of you here in class today." The line would probably be received only slightly better than something like, "I am so happy to see you all here today," when addressing a contingent of inmates at San Quentin prison.

What the speaker is doing with this approach is verbally patting the members of the audience on the back for being in attendance. With a little luck and a measure of skill, the speaker can make the listeners feel good about themselves, if only subconsciously.

I'm so happy to see you here today!

3.   Rhetorical question. A rhetorical question is a question to which the speaker really doesn't expect, nor want, an answer. Sometimes one question may be used in the attention step; sometimes a series of rhetorical questions may be used.

Let us set a scene to explore rhetorical questions. You are walking along a quiet residential street when suddenly a large dog springs from the bushes and takes a hunk out of your leg. A rhetorical question to open a speech might be, "Should dangerous animals be allowed to run at large, threatening anyone who crosses their path?" Followed by, "Should pedestrians be forced to carry whips and clubs to fend off attacks by uncontrolled animals?"

The rhetorical question is a form of reference to the subject, since it gives the audience a strong sense of what is coming in the speech.

6

4.   Quotation. A quotation appropriate to the subject matter is a common and recommended device in the attention step. But don't just sling the quotation out there—there is a definite technique used in presenting a quotation. State the author's name first, followed by his credentials, if necessary, so the audience won't be wondering who he or she was (or is). Now you can repeat the quotation. Do it this way: "President John F. Kennedy, in his inaugural address, said, 'Ask not what your country can do for you, but ask what you can do for your country.'"

Don't do it this way: "Comfort me with apples, for I am sick of love." Then, while you plow ahead with your presentation, the audience remains behind, trying to figure out who originated the quotation.

Here is the way to handle that quotation: "In the Bible—Proverbs to be exact—it says, 'Comfort me with apples, for I am sick of love.'" Then, continuing, you might follow with something like this: "I am sick of love in the library, in the parking lot across from the dormitory, under the stairs in the administration building. I am sick of being forced to avert my attention from scenes of passion everywhere I go. I am . . ."

The world is full of quotations and they are easy to find. At a library, you can locate a number of books that contain nothing but quotations. Further, the quotations are usually filed by subject matter, so finding something appropriate is not difficult. Ask a librarian.

In addition to being an excellent start for the attention step, quotations can be useful in the conclusion of a speech. Use them well and tastefully. It is possible to build an entire speech on quotations of others, but that's taking a good thing too far.

5.   Startling statement. The reason for using a startling statement to open a speech is to get your audience to make a noise—gasp or groan or whatever. Studies have shown that when people come into a group, they are psychologically separate individuals. If a speaker wants to lead that audience somewhere, he or she is going to have to meld all those individual minds into one collective mind.

6

Comfort me with apples, for I am sick of love.

A gasp or groan or some other exclamation is valuable because the gasper or groaner hears others gasping and groaning and knows they are of the same mind. The result is mental unity.

This is a technique long known to history's more successful rabble-rousers. The next time you see an old newsreel of Adolph Hitler addressing a huge gathering of his countrymen, watch closely. His harangues will be accompanied by thunderous outbursts from the audience in unison shouting, "Sieg Heil, Sieg Heil!" (an acclamation meaning "to victory!"). Although this was not used as a startling statement by the speaker, the general principle is the same—get the audience members all operating on the same wavelength by letting individuals know that the other members of the audience share their thoughts.

6

Beware!

Although the startling statement can be an effective device, be advised that it will not work on certain audiences. For example, there is no startling statement one can make that will elicit a gasp or groan from an audience of high school or college students. People of this age bracket are still developing their emotional structure, and they are very careful not to respond on a gut level. They are too busy being cool.

The startling statement works well with very young audiences. Picture the reaction of a kindergarten class if the speaker announced that Santa Claus was about to burst through the door. After a brief commotion, the youngsters would settle down to await the speaker's next words to find out what Santa was going to do once he was in the room.

Elderly people are also good subjects for the startling statement. Long ago they developed their self-confidence to a level that if they feel like gasping and groaning, they are going to do it. Announce to residents of a nursing home that their social security payments are going to be increased by 20 percent and see if there isn't a vocal reaction. See if they don't stop rocking and wait to hear more.

6

About this time you are thinking, "I bet I could come up with a statement that would get a reaction from a high school or college group." You are wrong—at least if you are thinking you would be using a startling statement. If you could say something strong enough to get a rise out of such a group, you have escalated from the startling statement to the "shocking statement." There is a difference.

Tell a college class that tuition is going to double next term. Tell a high school class that all boys will be required to get army haircuts and girls must wear ankle-length dresses and no makeup. You will get a reaction—you will get an explosion! But you will not, most likely, get full attention as you continue your speech. Your audience's minds will continue to chew on the shocking statement instead of following your presentation. A startling statement will further your speech; a shocking statement can stop it in its tracks.

6.   Humorous anecdote. You may well ask, "If a startling statement won't work with the high school and college crowd, what will?" The answer is a humorous anecdote, a joke. Tell an appropriate joke and you are on your way.

A joke has the same purpose as a startling statement. The idea is to gain a vocal reaction from your audience in order to bring them together. But instead of a gasp or groan (unless your story is too raunchy or corny) the vocal reaction will be a laugh.

There are two guidelines to use in selecting a joke for your attention step: (1) It must be strongly related to your topic. A story about an inebriated brain surgeon would be inappropriate for a speech about growing petunias. (2) The story must not be too ripe for the audience. They may laugh and will probably continue laughing while you are trying to get on with your presentation. In fact, they may snicker about the opening joke throughout your speech and not hear another thing you say. Worse yet, you may offend some members of the audience, and their minds will snap shut and remain so until you leave the podium.

Libraries have many books full of jokes, all indexed by topic and for the use of speakers. If you will be facing an audience of people in their late teens or early 20s, see if you can come up with some appropriate stories. Ask a librarian.

7.   Illustration. Use the illustration often; it can work better than any of the other six methods. An illustration is a story about things that have happened to you or to people you know.

Here is an example of a powerful attention step for speaking about the burn center of a hospital:

6

One morning when I was 10 years old, I was awakened by the smell of smoke. I leaped from my bed, threw open the bedroom door, and was engulfed by a sheet of flames. The last thing I remember is the smell of my own flesh burning.

The firemen were able to drag me from the fire and take me to the burn center at St. Luke's Hospital. I later learned that I was one of the most badly burned people who ever survived his injuries. I not only survived, but because of the skill and the care of the doctors and nurses at St. Luke's, today I am living a normal, full life.

➤ THE NEED-PROPOSITION STEP

In an upcoming chapter on the persuasive speech, you'll learn that the need step is tremendously important. For the present, however, you'll see that the need step in informative speeches is only half of one sentence and tells the members of the audience why they need to listen.

Any need step can be categorized in two ways:

1. The members of the audience will listen to your presentation because you are about to tell them something they need to know: "Ladies and gentlemen, because our airplane is about to crash in downtown Burbank, I am going to tell you how to put on and operate a parachute."

2. The audience members will want to listen to you because you will speak on something you enjoy and want to share with them. "Because I know a lot of you are interested in starting your own businesses, let me tell you about the informative meeting I just went to explaining how to get financing, initiate the necessary paperwork, and figure out the city ordinances on small businesses."

6

The proposition is found in the second half of the sentence that begins with the need step. The proposition is a specific statement that tells the audience exactly what is going to be covered in the body of the speech. Look at the above need-proposition combination that states, "Because I know a lot of you are interested in starting your own businesses (need), let me tell you about the informative meeting I just went to explaining how to get financing, initiate the necessary paperwork, and figure out the city ordinances on small businesses (proposition)." Do not place the proposition in the forepart of the sentence and the need step at the end. It will sound odd.

Just to set the need-proposition combination in your minds, here are a few more examples:

- Because I want you to learn from my experience (need), I am going to tell you the causes of three of my worst car wrecks (proposition).

- Because I love basketball (need), today I would like to explain the difference between zone and man-to-man defense (proposition).

- Because I want you all to try skiing this winter (need), I want to tell you how clothing you already have in your closet will substitute for expensive ski togs (proposition).

- Because I did not want to take this course either (need), I am going to tell you about three strategies I use to get safely through the class with a minimum of effort (proposition).

➤ SATISFACTION STEP

The satisfaction step is the main part of the speech—the easy part. All you have to do is tell the audience what you said you were going to tell them when you stated the proposition. The satisfaction step is made up of a sufficient number of one-point speeches to cover the topic stated in the proposition.

For example, recall the proposition, "I am going to tell you the causes of three of my worst car wrecks." Obviously, you are going to have to have three one-point speeches to cover this, as in the following examples:

- My first car wreck happened when a tire blew out. (Of course, the speaker would expand as necessary on this.)

- My second car wreck was caused when another vehicle ran a stop sign. (And expand.)

- The cause of my third car wreck is a little hazy in my mind, because I was too sleepy to remember it very well.

Notice that these (abbreviated) one-point speeches have satisfied the proposition, which stated, "I am going to tell you the cause of my three worst car wrecks." Do not offer information not promised in the proposition. The audience will become confused and their attention will wander.

➤ THE CONCLUSION STEP

No matter what the length of the speech, it must have a conclusion and that conclusion must be short. There is nothing worse than hearing someone say, "In conclusion . . ." and then rattle on for another five minutes. For the informative speech, start the conclusion by restating the proposition and adding a sentence or so behind it: "Today I have told you about the causes of my three worst car wrecks. I hope that someday you may recall what I said and perhaps avoid an accident of your own."

6

. . . .

Summary

Understanding the motivated sequence will give you the skills to present effective informative speeches. The key steps to the motivated sequence for informative speeches are:

1. Attention step.

2. Need-proposition step.

3. Satisfaction step.

4. Conclusion step.

Keep in mind that not every audience will respond to the same attention-getting openers or identify with the language you use to present your ideas. Remember to tailor your speech material to your audience's needs and expectations. As we've said before, practice, practice, practice until you feel more comfortable and confident.

Skill Builder

Create five topics for informative speeches. Each topic should be stated as a full sentence, using the need–proposition format. Examples:

1. "Because my teachers in grade school deeply influenced my life, I am going to tell you about my most hated teacher, my favorite teacher, and the teacher for whom I was willing to work the hardest." Notice that the proposition tells the audience exactly how many one-point speeches will be in the satisfaction step of the speech.

2. "Because it is a decision many adults here must make, I am going to tell you the advantages and disadvantages of owning a car in the city." Notice that the audience knows what to expect from your speech by what you tell them in the proposition.

   • Read one or more of your need-proposition sentences to the class to make sure you have clearly communicated the intent of your speech. Listen and use the feedback you get from your classmates.

   • Deliver an informative speech to the class. Speeches should be five to seven minutes long:

   1. Attention step—about two minutes.

   2. Need-proposition sentence—three to five seconds.

   3. Satisfaction step—about one and a half minutes per one-point speech.

   4. Conclusion—30 seconds.

- Critique each other's informative speeches. Take careful notes during each speech and be sure to word suggestions for improvement in a positive manner.

6

Seven

THE DEMONSTRATION SPEECH AND VISUAL AIDS

- Understand that a demonstration speech is simply an informative speech with visual aids.

- Learn to use various visual aids to maximize their effectiveness.

- Realize that delivering and listening to speeches can be fun.

1
2
3
4
5
6
7
8
9

The demonstration speech gives you an opportunity to unlock your imagination and let it run freely over some of those "best" topic ideas that have been simmering in the back of your mind. This type of speech is perfectly named — the speaker gives hands-on demonstrations of a skill or craft. Speaking to an audience about something you know well is a great opportunity to practice your speaking skills in an informal setting.

And a demonstration speech can be the speech that you will be remembered by: "Joe Smith? Sure I remember him. He's the one who set the classroom on fire during his welding demonstration."

[SETTING THE STAGE]

Demonstration speeches can be made in just about any location, under any circumstances. Many classes have seen the classroom furniture stacked in a corner to make way for a gymnastics demonstration. Some classes have seen a demonstration of how to navigate a city street map, or how to entertain kids on a rainy day. Some find themselves outside, learning how to saddle a horse. And one miserable winter day at 6:30 A.M., a class was huddled in a frigid barn, watching demonstrations of rodeo events.

Props (equipment or visual aids) can vary from the usual classroom charts and pictures to the bizarre and exotic. Medical students at one college would occasionally bring a cadaver to class to show their classmates the workings of the color-coded intestines. Sportsminded students may lead a contingent of their colleagues to the gymnasium or other appropriate place in order to demonstrate some type of athletic prowess. Demonstrations of culinary skills are often greatly appreciated, especially if there is a sampling session connected with the presentation. Use your imagination—the stage belongs to you!

7

[ALERTING THE SENSES]

The demonstration speech is, in essence, an informative speech. It employs any number of items or devices to appeal to and stimulate the audience's five senses: touch, smell, hearing, sight, and taste.

Let's envision what a speaker whose topic is making home-made fudge might do. She walks into class carrying a handsome platter laden with walnut-decorated pieces of fudge. The candy is still warm and exudes an intoxicating aroma of chocolate. The speaker then distributes a piece of fudge to each class member before giving the presentation.

What senses are involved? Obviously, the sense of sight, but not only because of the visual attractiveness of the fudge. The audience also watches the speaker and is stimulated by her appearance, her mannerisms, her gestures.

The sense of taste plays a powerful part in this presentation. The sense of smell is also important—what's more alluring than the scent of warm chocolate?

Hearing, of course, is dependent upon the speaker's voice and what she says—unless she has concocted a fudge that goes, "snap, crackle, pop."

The sense of touch? We all know the surprising contrast between the creamy smoothness of chocolate and the crunch of walnuts.

The above example leads us to believe, probably correctly, that an audience so stimulated is going to hang on the speaker's every word. The more sensual stimulation a speaker employs, the better the speech will be received.

[THE MOTIVATED SEQUENCE FOR DEMONSTRATION SPEECHES]

Demonstration speeches, just like informative speeches, can be broken down into the steps of a motivated sequence. By following these steps, you'll be able to clearly outline and plan your speech.

7

For **demonstration speeches** with visual aids, you'll use a modified version of the motivated sequence. The steps you'll follow here are:

- Attention step.
- Need-proposition sentence.
- Satisfaction step.
- Conclusion step.

➤ ATTENTION STEP

Your demonstration speech should include a thought-provoking or humorous attention-grabber. Look back at the last chapter to refresh your memory on the many ways you can get your audience to sit up and pay attention. Your attention step should last about two minutes. In the demonstration speech, you've got a head start on attracting attention through your props or visual aids. It's hard not to notice the smell of warm fudge!

➤ NEED-PROPOSITION SENTENCE

Express your simple need–proposition sentence, "Because everyone seems to like this fudge, today I'm going to show you how easy it is to make," and start demonstrating. You'll be so busy showing off your skills and talents, you may not even notice that you're also practicing good speaking habits!

➤ SATISFACTION STEP

In the satisfaction step, the presentation will be directed by the wording of the proposition, which said, "Today I am going to show you how easy it [the fudge] is to make." Remember, the speaker is responsible for whatever she said in the proposition — for expanding on it, for giving useful information about it. If anything is left out of the satisfaction step, if it does not deliver the information promised in the proposition, the audience will be unhappy and stop listening.

7

. . . .
Don't stand in front of your visual aids.

[VISUAL AIDS: USE YOUR PROPS!]

Visual aids can be anything from movies to mousetraps that will help to inform or to hold the interest of an audience.

Perhaps the most common visual aid used in a basic speech class is a chart that complements the speaker's verbal information. Charts will often show statistics (numbers) or outline topics. The visual aid may only supplement a speech, or it may be the topic of a speech.

For example, if the speaker is making a presentation on the number of traffic accidents during the past year, a chart showing

7

the number of these accidents would be a valuable supplement. The speech is not about the chart—the chart only helps the audience understand the speech.

Sometimes the visual aid itself might be the topic. Let's suppose the speaker is showing the audience how to operate a camera. He would bring the camera to class, show the audience how to open it, how to insert and advance the film, and how to make the proper lens and speed settings.

There are several things to consider when designing a visual aid. Obviously, the audience must be able to see it. Don't stand in front of it. If you are using a chart, make it large enough to be seen by those in the very back of the room. But suppose you are talking about a piece of jewelry—a ring. How is the audience going to see this tiny object? Here's how you do it. Verbally describe the item; tell the story behind it. Give the audience all the information they need about the ring. Once you have done this, let the audience members pass the ring among themselves. This can be done very quickly because they already know what they are looking for and only need hold the ring for a few seconds before passing it on. If you are still talking, chances are the audience will be listening because the ring, if presented as described, will not be a distraction.

Speaking of distraction: Do not let your visual aid distract the audience from what you are saying. If a person were speaking about building a fire in the wilderness and then set the room on fire during the presentation, many audience members would be distracted.

When the time comes to make the speech with the help of visual aids, you'll be teaching one another. Watch what works and does not work for others. See the results of the imagination some of your classmates devote to constructing a visual aid. Appreciate the incredible ingenuity of the human mind as the array of visual aids opens in front of you.

In later years, when you are on the job and asked to make a presentation, you are going to remember the visual aids you saw in speech class. And by remembering, your own imagination will be stimulated to select marvelous material for your own presentation.

➤ CONCLUSION STEP

The conclusion can probably be handled in 30 or 45 seconds. Many speakers will begin a conclusion by slightly rewording the proposition: "Today I have told you about how easy it is to make this delightful fudge." It is also proper and beneficial to summarize the main points of the satisfaction step.

(Remember the "army" method of giving a speech — "Tell 'em what you're gonna tell 'em, tell 'em, and tell 'em what you told 'em.)

Very often the conclusion of demonstration speech ends with an invitation to the audience members:

"Come over to my house and we'll make some fudge."

"Talk to me after class and I can give you more information on going through a job interview."

"If we had more time, I could tell you how to use the other features of this city map."

In the demonstration speech, the speaker may merely show the audience an object or objects, such as the fudge, and talk about it. Or the speaker could actually show (demonstrate) how that fudge is made by whipping up a batch. In a demonstration speech, a speaker may bring a chain saw and tell how useful it is for cutting timber. Or he could start the chain saw and show how it works, perhaps by partitioning the podium!

[DISASTER LURKS]

As mentioned in previous chapters, practice is necessary. Handling visual aids can be awkward if not carefully planned.

7

One student studying to be a veterinary assistant was showing how to draw blood from a mouse. She had done this successfully in class and knew the procedure. But she forgot to practice her speech with a mouse.

Her introduction went beautifully, her need-proposition was perfect, but when she picked up the mouse, it bit her on the thumb.

Undaunted, the resourceful speaker then explained that a great deal of care must be taken to restrain animals before blood is drawn.

So she demonstrated the restraint method, picked up the syringe—and again was bitten.

At this point, she was bleeding so profusely she had to give up the effort.

Cooking provides infinite opportunity for disaster.

An apprentice bartender decided to share with the class his expertise in making strawberry daiquiris with a kitchen blender. At the last minute, he decided the instructor might not allow rum in class, so he substituted water. Without the antifreeze quality of the rum, the mixture froze solid.

The cake of ice stripped the gears on the blender and refused to pour from the pitcher. Not only was the blender destroyed, but so was the speech.

Always practice with your visual aids!

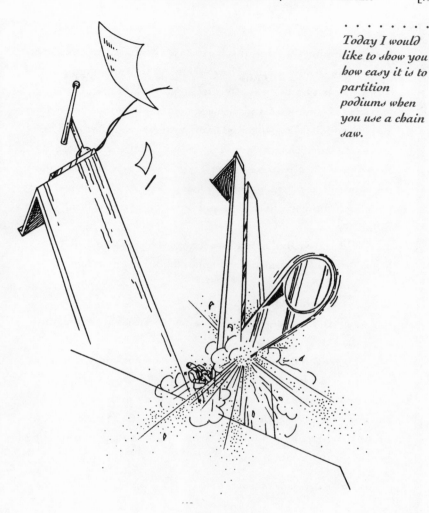

Today I would like to show you how easy it is to partition podiums when you use a chain saw.

[ADVICE FROM AN EXPERT]

Remember the woman in an earlier chapter who could not give a "speech" but could give a "talk"? Now, after many years of experience, she has become an accomplished speaker. Here is what she has to say about visual aids.

It is my opinion that the message one is trying to convey is driven home more firmly, retained longer, and is more meaningful when supplemented by the use of visual aids. A training quiz that the participant completes and discusses during lecture time is much more beneficial than a printed handout to be read later on. Use of a video to enhance or augment narrative is much more beneficial than one or the other used alone. I try to use those aids that allow for immediate learning and feedback. Each time I schedule a training or information meeting, I try to employ one or all of the following:

a.   Video (to supplement or enhance the spoken words).

b.   Written handout requiring immediate reading and completion.

c.   Written handout to be read later.

d.   Reference materials (to be taken and used at some later date).

e.   Overhead projector (presents an excellent opportunity to interject humor).

The choice of visual aid(s) primarily depends on the applicability, the size of the room, the size of the group, and the makeup of the group participants. Another factor that also may have some bearing is the location selected.

Mazie Brandt, National College, Rapid City, South Dakota

7

☞ Summary

Demonstration speeches provide a great opportunity to sharpen your speaking skills in front of a group. Basically, demonstration speeches are informative speeches with an added element — visual aids, or props. Effective demonstration speeches rely on the use of good props to demonstrate whatever you want to explain to your audience.

Feel free (within reason!) to use all sorts of visual aids to make your point to your listeners. Remember that the best way to use visual aids in a demonstration speech is to make them a smooth part of your presentation — don't let your props overwhelm you or distract from your message.

Skill Builder

Prepare, complete with visual aids, a 10- to 12-minute demonstration speech. (Note that this may be a time-consuming process.) Set aside class time for delivering these presentations. After each day's presentations, discuss the speeches among your classmates.

By this time, you're already experienced and skilled in the discussion and critique process. Be alert, constructively critical, and helpful.

7

Eight

[
THE

PERSUASIVE

SPEECH
]

- Learn three types of persuasive speeches.

- Learn how to construct each of these three types.

- Learn how to prove a point.

1

2

3

4

5

6

7

8

9

The persuasive speech leads the audience to agree with your point of view. For each point of view in a persuasive speech, there is an opposite point of view. If you're going to advocate a certain course of action, it must be remembered that someone else could advocate a different, or opposite, course of action. "We should fix the streets now." "We should delay fixing the streets."

As the speaker, you must choose one side or the other of these pro-con pairs. If there is no argument, no disagreement, there would be no need to present a persuasive speech.

There are three major types of persuasive speeches. They are called proposition of policy, proposition of value, *and* proposition of fact. *Each type has a number of substeps based largely on the motivated sequence discussed earlier in this book. However, in a persuasive speech, the need step now stands on its own; the proposition is now a free-standing statement.*

The components of the motivated sequence as used in the persuasive proposition of policy speech are:

- *Attention step.*
- *Need step.*
- *Proposition.*
- *Satisfaction step.*
- *Visualization step.*
- *Action step.*

Note that the visualization step is a new twist on the standard motivated sequence you first learned in Chapter 6.

. . . .

[PROPOSITION OF POLICY:]
[CHANGE THE STATUS QUO]

8

The key to recognizing proposition of policy is the use of the word "should." "The United States *should* put a manned spaceship on Jupiter." "The city council *should* repair the streets."

➤ ATTENTION STEP

The first step of the motivated sequence in the proposition of policy is the attention step. This will be composed of perhaps two or three one-point speeches; an illustration or quotation is often the opening statement. Next in the attention step is a definition of terms, to give the audience some background information, followed by a discussion of the way things are *today*—the present situation. Let's give an example of items that might be included in the attention step.

Quotation: "The president of the local association of tire dealers says, 'This spring was the best sales period we have ever had, due to the severe tire damage caused by potholes in the streets.'"

Definition of terms: "A pothole is a hole in the pavement, usually caused by severe freezing conditions, or heavy traffic, or both. Large potholes can cause tire damage."

The present situation: "Today, the streets of Centerville are full of potholes caused by the severe winter."

(The whole thrust of a proposition of policy hinges on the "present situation." Some people refer to this as the "status quo." The way that material in the proposition of policy speech is presented is based on whether you, the speaker, want to *change* the status quo or to *maintain* the status quo: no change.)

➤ NEED STEP

In a speech to change the status quo, the need step lists the problems resulting from the present situation. The need step is presented in the negative, a series of one-point speeches that tell the bad points of the present situation. For example:

"Because of the sorry condition of the streets, motorists are experiencing considerable damage to the tires and suspension systems of their automobiles. The potential for accidents is increased because of uneven street surfaces. If the streets are not repaired soon, the deterioration will occur at an even more rapid rate as traffic and moisture continue to take their toll."

8

A pothole is a hole in the pavement, often caused by freezing.

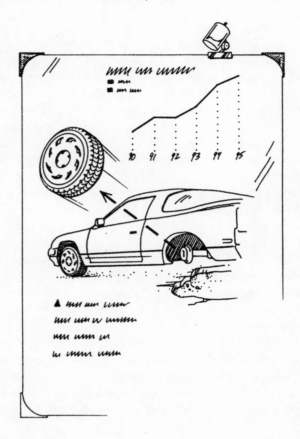

➤ PROPOSITION

The proposition would then be, "The city should initiate a program to repair the streets."

➤ SATISFACTION STEP

The satisfaction step offers the solution to the problem. It comes in two parts—what to do and how to do it: "The city street department must begin work as soon as possible to fill potholes and resurface streets where necessary. To raise money for the project, the city should immediately increase the local sales tax by one-half cent."

8

➤ VISUALIZATION STEP

The visualization (or VIZ) step tells the results, or the benefits, that will occur when the speaker's recommended course of action is followed. "If the streets are fixed, motorists will save a great deal of money on automobile repairs, and the danger of accidents will be reduced. Prompt action will prevent further deterioration of the streets, thereby saving considerable money in the future."

➤ ACTION STEP

The action step is the conclusion of the proposition of policy speeches. This step summarizes the strongest portion of the speech, either the satisfaction or the visualization (VIZ) step. In this speech, it is probable that the VIZ step would be the most powerful: Save damage to your car, save money, reduce accidents, and prevent continuing street damage.

The speech always ends with a request for action on the part of audience members. You want their help in getting a sales tax increase so the streets may be repaired. You might ask them to persuade their friends and neighbors to vote for a tax increase. You might encourage them to discuss the problem with their city council representatives.

[PROPOSITION OF POLICY: MAINTAIN THE STATUS QUO]

In a proposition of policy to *maintain* the status quo, the same topic could be developed by another speaker who has the opposite point of view. In either case, the attention step would be the same. The present situation does not change.

➤ NEED STEP

If the speaker wants to maintain the status quo, he will develop problems, but he will use the problems to illustrate what will happen in the future if the proposed changes are made. Usually

8

the problems are developed in a cause-effect relationship: "If we do this, so-and-so will result."

➤ PROPOSITION

The proposition (again, a proposal) would sound like, "The city should refrain from repairing the streets at this time."

➤ SATISFACTION STEP

The plan (what and how) would describe some way to prevent change from the present situation from occurring. In other words, the plan would maintain the status quo. In most cases, some type of program to educate the public is the first step of this plan.

➤ VISUALIZATION STEP

This would be the benefits we have now, with no change.

➤ ACTION STEP

This summarizes the satisfaction step or the VIZ step and requests the audience's help in starting on the plan.

[PROPOSITION OF VALUE SPEECH]

The proposition of value format is used to make comparisons of either tangible or intangible subjects: that is, to compare either things or ideas. The goal, of course, is to convince the audience to accept the thing or idea favored by the speaker. For example, which automobile would be best for the college student—the Belchfire V8 or the Economobile?

The **proposition of value speech** uses these steps of the motivated sequence:

• Attention step.

• Need step.

8

- Proposition.
- Visualization step.
- Action step.

➤ ATTENTION STEP

The first part of the attention step is, obviously, to get the audience's attention. Then, the speaker must establish the value of whatever the subject is. Example: "What values should a college student look for in an automobile? College students need a car that has a large cargo space (to carry stuff from home), good gas mileage because they need their money for tuition, and they need a car with a low incidence of repair."

➤ NEED STEP

The need step, using the criteria (values) listed in the attention step, lists the disadvantages of the Belchfire. For example, the cargo space of the Belchfire is barely large enough for the spare tire. The Belchfire has a high price. It gets terrible gasoline mileage. It has a bad repair record.

➤ PROPOSITION

The proposition is, then, that college students would be better off with an Economobile than a Belchfire.

➤ VISUALIZATION STEP

The visualization step should deal with the advantages that accrue to the college student who owns an Economobile. For every disadvantage of the Belchfire, as listed in the need step, list the opposite corresponding advantage of the Economobile. Whereas the Belchfire's initial price is high, the Economobile is quite reasonable. Economobiles get great gas mileage, they seldom need repair, and their cargo space is very large in proportion to the overall size of the vehicle.

8

➤ ACTION STEP

The action step, or the conclusion, follows easily. Summarize the viualization step by telling how great the Economobile is and tell the audience to run right out and buy one.

Note there should be no negative material after the need steps in these two formats. You cannot prove a negative, and your speech would end up spiraling downward.

[PROPOSITION OF FACT SPEECH]

In a proposition of fact speech, the speaker will clear up misconceptions that are held by his audience. He will use any of several kinds of proof to overcome the misconceptions.

The **proposition of fact persuasive speech** is based on the following steps of the motivated sequence:

• Attention step.

• Need step.

• Proposition.

• Satisfaction step.

• Action step.

➤ ATTENTION STEP

The initial step deals with the history of the subject. As an example, let's choose a notorious bad man as the subject for our presentation:

"Jesse James, the famous outlaw, was born in western Missouri September 5, 1847, the son of a Baptist minister. His career in crime began December 7, 1869, when he robbed a Missouri bank. In 1873, the James Gang graduated from banks to train robbery when they held up a Rock Island train near Council Bluffs, Iowa.

"After 1873, the James Gang was spotted in Texas, Montana, Colorado, and Arkansas, but most of its activities were in Missouri and Iowa.

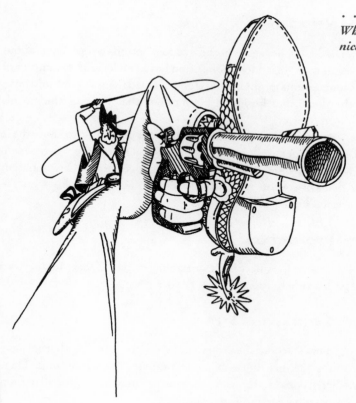

Who sez I ain't a nice guy?

"In 1882, James, his wife, and two children were living in St. Joseph, Missouri, where he used the name Thomas Howard. He died April 3 of that year when he was shot in the back of the head by Robert (the dirty little coward*) Ford.

"During and after his career as an outlaw, legends grew up about Jesse James, many of which alleged that he was a good man. I am going to prove that Jesse James was not a good man, but a man who spent his life wallowing in all kinds of reprehensible activities."

*Within days of Jesse James' death, one Billy Gashade wrote "The Ballad of Jesse James," a song that was to haunt Robert Ford the rest of his life. A sample verse:

　It was Robert Ford, that dirty little coward,
　I wonder how he does feel,
　For he ate of Jesse's bread and he slept in Jesse's bed,
　And he laid Jesse James in his grave.

8

➤ NEED STEP

In a need step, list some of the misconceptions people hold about Jesse James, misconceptions often based on legend. Examples of misconceptions might be that Jesse robbed from the rich and gave to the poor, that he loved his mother, that he was kind to his children.

At this point, the speaker will find it profitable to show these misconceptions on a chart, using two or three key words each. However, do not develop these misconceptions. Development can backfire—you may strengthen the audience's hold on the misconceptions.

➤ PROPOSITION

The proposition is: "I am going to prove that Jesse was a dirty, lowdown, lying crook."

➤ SATISFACTION STEP

This step satisfies the proposition by proving that misconceptions are just that—misconceptions. They are wrong. There are three types of proof, and the speaker may use any or all of them in disproving each misconception:

1.   **Statistics.** Use them sparingly. Write them down so you won't forget them or make a mistake. "Documentation obtained from the outlaw's corporate books shows that, during 1875, Jesse James and his gang robbed 14 trains, making off with $97,248.55. That same year, Jesse and his gang spent $98,772.33 in saloons, card houses, and other places of low entertainment. Late that year, county records show, Kate's Pleasure Palace in St. Louis filed a collection suit against Jesse in the amount of $1,523.78 for nonpayment of his account there. In other words, statistics show us that Jesse's expenditures exceeded his income. There was no other money left over to be distributed to the poor. These statistics further indicate that Jesse's off-duty activities were not as high-minded as some believe."

2.   **Expert opinion** states the credentials of the person upon whose opinion you are going to rely in proving your point.

8

Make sure the person is really an expert. Here is a hypothetical example: "John Elwood Forbes, history professor emeritus of the University of Missouri, has made a life-long study of Jesse James and his gang. Forbes has authored 17 books on these outlaws and has written what is considered by many to be the most comprehensive biography of Jesse."

Now would be the appropriate time to use some of John Elwood Forbes's opinions to refute some of the misconceptions:

"Ever since he was a child, Jesse James was unable to establish a benevolent relationship with his mother. When he was young, she beat him with great regularity (with a stout hickory branch). When Jesse reached sufficient physical size, he removed the hickory branch from his mother's gnarled hand and spent the next 16 years beating knobs on her withering body. This penchant for violence carried over into his relations with his own children, and they, too, often felt the force of the hickory."*

3. **Historical proof** often deals with an occurrence in the past that, human nature being what it is, is likely to happen in the future; or conversely, something that today's scientists know to be true and is used to explain something that happened in the past.

For example, Jesse James' imagined strenuous relations with his mother and then his children can be explained by today's theories of child abuse; that is, the abused child will grow into an abusing parent. Further, it has been theorized that an abused child has a tendency to develop criminal inclinations.

Historical proof can be based on your own experience — a story about something that has happened to you in the past. If it happened to you, this proves it could happen again in the future.

➤ ACTION STEP

In the action step, the speaker will summarize his rebuttals to misconceptions that appear in the satisfaction step. This speaker is not particularly trying to sell the audience a product; he is

---

*Author's note: The information on Jesse James, from his birth in 1845 until his death in April of 1882, is true. The remainder, including Forbes' imaginary "facts" about Jesse James' lifestyle and treatment of his mother and children, is actually contrary to historical reports. He treated his children well and his mother, too, although she was a very difficult person. (James was by no means a saint — he admitted to murdering seventeen people who got in his way.) Thus Forbes' "expert" testimony does not stand up to scrutiny.

8

merely seeking their agreement. A typical closing statement might be "With the information I have given you, I am sure you will agree that Jesse James is not the good man the legends portray."

[OUTLINING A SPEECH]

For those of you who are lazy (and what thinking person isn't?), there is an easy way to prepare a speech to persuade. If you analyze the preceding information, you will deduce that once you had (1) set up the proposition and (2) decided which of the three types of proposition it is, the rest is practically an exercise in filling in the blanks.

As an example, let's assume the speaker is constructing a proposition of policy to change the status quo. The topic is a change of tuition.

Here is how such a speech might be outlined:

I.   Attention step.
   A.   Give a history of how tuition rates have grown over the years at Green City Community College.
   B.   Define what costs are involved in the operation of the college.
   C.   Review the present situation; use statistics that show the costs of operating Green City Community College are outstripping income from tuition.
II. Need step (outline problems the above situation is causing).
   A.   The college is going to run out of operating money.
   B.   New instructional materials are needed now.
   C.   Building maintenance has been delayed, resulting in a poor environment for students.
   Proposition: "Green City Community College should increase tuition beginning summer quarter."
III. Satisfaction step (this is where the speaker presents a plan to accomplish the aim stated in the proposition).
   A.   What: Increase revenue by 10 percent.
   B.   How: Students will be charged one half of the increase and the balance will come from instructor salaries.

8

IV. Visualization (VIZ) step (list benefits of increased tuition).
    A.   The cash flow of the college will be improved and the college can pay some bills and purchase new instructional materials.
    B.   Needed maintenance can be accomplished.
V. Action step.
    A.   Summarize the VIZ step.
    B.   Ask the audience to sign a petition in favor of the tuition increase.

If someone in the audience disagrees with the above speech, he or she might prepare and deliver a proposition of policy to *maintain* the status quo. "Green City Community College *should* keep tuition rates where they are." This speech would be outlined as follows:

I.   Attention step (this would be the same as in the previous speech).
II.   Need step (state problems that would occur in the *future* if tuition is increased).
    A.   An increase would cause some students to drop out.
    B.   Lower enrollment will mean less money to spend on maintenance.
    C.   When the campus begins to look shabby, fewer students will want to enroll.
    D.   With fewer and fewer students, the college will fail.
    Proposition: "Green City Community College should keep its tuition rates where they are now."
III.   VIZ step (list benefits if tuition is held at the current level).
    A.   Students currently in school will be able to stay in school and graduate.
    B.   They will encourage their friends to enroll.
    C.   Increased enrollment will lead to an increase in income.
V.   Action step.
    A.   Summarize the satisfaction or the VIZ step.
    B.   Request students to make the administrators aware of the situation as they view it.

8

Below is a sample outline of the proposition of value, wherein the speaker is trying to convince audience members that it is better to get an education in a small, private career college than in a large university.

I.   Attention step.
   A.   Discuss the difficulty of choosing a college.
   B.   List things that are important to a student:
      1.   Personal attention from instructors.
      2.   Making friends.
      3.   Small classes.
      4.   Opportunity to participate in many activities.
II. Need step (list a disadvantage found at a large university for each of the qualities mentioned in B, above).
Proposition: "It is better to get your education at a small private career college than at a large university."
III. VIZ step (for each of the disadvantages in the need step, state a corresponding advantage found at a small private career college).
IV. Action step (summarize the advantages of the small college, and request that each member of the audience advise friends and relatives of the merits of the small college).

If a speaker wishes to present the opposite point of view, he could do it by establishing a different set of values in the attention step and then developing the speech from there.

(Included in a different set of values could be such factors as the cost of tuition, the quality of instruction, and the availability of resources offered by a large university.)

As an example of an outline for a proposition of fact persuasive speech, let us advocate that it is beneficial for students to work while they are attending college.

I.   Attention step (give a brief history of student employment in colleges, starting from the beginning when there was no involvement by the college, through today when colleges are heavily involved in finding jobs for their students).
II. Need step (list misconceptions that people often hold).
   A.   A student can make enough money on work-study to pay all education expenses.

B.   A job would cut into study time.

C.   A student with a job cannot participate in school activities.

D.   A student who holds a job will be burned out by the time he graduates.

Proposition: "Today I am going to prove that students who work while in college are more successful as students and in their careers after graduation."

III.   Satisfaction step (disprove each of the misconceptions, using any combination of statistical proof, proof through expert opinion, and historical proof).

A.   Examples of statistical proof:

    1.   At Acme College during the years 1979 to 1983, 73 percent of the students were employed, according to a survey conducted by the college.

    2.   Of those students working, 59 percent were consistently on the dean's list.

B.   Example of proof by expert opinion: According to Guy W. Tillet, dean of student services at National College in Rapid City, South Dakota, "The students who accept or require work are generally more successful in college and career development after college. The additional responsibilities of work require that the student carefully budget and use time. Use of time is critical for success in college and in career development at any point in life."

C.   Example of historical proof: (use stories of the success of others or of your own). "I am in my third year of college now and I have always had a part-time job. It was often difficult to reconcile demands made upon my time by both my work and my studies, so I was forced to budget my time wisely. I knew there was only so much time to do homework so I could not waste it. Because of these time constraints, I had to work hard and fast and with concentration. As a result, my grade point average has never fallen below 3.3."

8

IV. Action step (summarize the satisfaction step and end with a request that the audience agree with the proposition): "With the information I have given you, I am sure you will agree that students who work while in college are more successful in their education and in their careers after graduation."

To reiterate, construction of a persuasive speech is quite easy. All you have to do is write down your proposition, decide which of the three types it is, and then organize the speech based on the examples just given.

Having mastered organization of the persuasive speech, there is only one more necessary ingredient in the art of persuasion—documentation and proof.

$\left[\text{PROVE IT}\right]$

Documentation states where or from whom you received your information. If you got it from your own knowledge, you must state your credentials—explain how you know what you know. Use documentation to substantiate the three kinds of proof—historical, statistical, or expert opinion.

Each item of proof, along with its documentation, can be written on a notecard, but only one item per card. Documentation notecard examples are shown below.

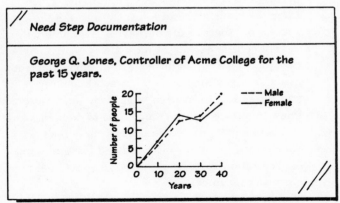

Use in the need step of proposition of fact speech.

```
┌─────────────────────────────────────────────────┐
│ //  Satisfaction Step Documentation              │
│ ┌─────────────────────────────────────────────┐ │
│ │ Mike M., now a senior student at Acme College:│ │
│ │  "My parents did not want me to work my       │ │
│ │  senior year and because of lack of           │ │
│ │  discipline my grades were terrible. I have   │ │
│ │  since held a part-time job and my grades     │ │
│ │  have improved drastically. I have learned to │ │
│ │  use my time."                                │ │
│ └─────────────────────────────────────────────┘ │
│                                            //    │
└─────────────────────────────────────────────────┘
```

Use in the visualization step of the proposition of policy speech.

Follow the documentation and proof process through each of the steps of a persuasive speech. The exceptions are action steps and, in the proposition of fact speech, the need step.

. . . .

Summary

This chapter has shown you how to convince others to share your opinions. The psychological impact of persuasive speeches could make them the most valuable type of speech for you to master.

Keep this book for future reference at school, at home, on the job—anytime you want to persuade someone that your ideas are valid and worthwhile. Practice and refine your persuasive speaking skills so you can convince anyone of almost anything!

Skill Builders

1. It's Your Turn

All radio and television ads are based on one of the three types of persuasive speeches. This exercise will help you get to the root of advertising's persuasive techniques.

Watch television or listen to the radio long enough to observe 10 commercials, and write a brief description of what happens in each.

Then, during the next class period, take turns describing some of the commercials and discussing their persuasive techniques. See if you can write the outline of a persuasive speech based on one of the commercials you've analyzed.

Go one step further and present a persuasive speech based on this outline — in essence you're putting yourselves in the role of advertisers at an initial "concept" meeting. Can the persuasive message or feeling of the advertisement be expressed clearly in an organized persuasive speech?

(Instructors should be aware there will only be time for two or three of these exercises and discussions during a class period.)

2.   Putting It All Together

This will be the easiest assignment of all because it is the *only* speech you will give in which there will be no new material.

By now you should have several "hot" topics in mind, either opposing speeches heard in class or some other topic, perhaps something from the newspaper.

Your assignment is to prepare a 15- to17-minute speech to persuade with full documentation and proof, using visual aids for most of the material. (Remember, charts can make good notecards for you and the audience.)

8

Nine

$$[\quad \text{SPEAK} \quad \text{UP} \quad \text{FOR} \quad \text{YOURSELF} \quad]$$

By studying this chapter, you will:

- Develop useful speaking skills for a job interview.

- Learn effective telephone techniques.

- Learn to introduce a speaker and graciously accept an award or honor.

The types of speeches we've covered so far—one-point, demonstration, informative, and persuasive—will serve you well in most situations where you need to present a speech for an audience. Usually, you'll have a specific purpose for giving one of these types of speeches, and you'll have time to consider your topic, your audience, and your speech organization. But what happens when you need to speak off the cuff and still sound thoughtful and prepared? In a job interview, on the phone at work, and when you are introducing someone to a group of people, speaking effectively can really pay off. Are you starting to get nervous and sweat a bit under the collar? Well, never fear, because this chapter will give you the tools to remain calm, cool, and collected in these situations.

[THE JOB INTERVIEW]

Interviewing for a job is one of the most important tests of your speaking skill. After all, an interview for a job you really want could be the best showcase for your talents. An interview is your chance to make an impression on your future employers—make the most of this opportunity. Although you may feel that there's no way to prepare for the speaking you'll do in an interview—each interview is unique—there are certain ways to prepare.

➤ LOOK LIKE YOU MEAN IT

Before you go to the interview, make sure you're dressed appropriately for the type of job you're applying for. It's a good idea to visit the office or work site to see how other employees are dressed. If you're applying for a construction job, don't wear high heels. If you're applying for an office job, leave your combat boots at home. A good rule of thumb is to dress as neatly and simply as you can.

9

Avoid splashy colors or attention-getting jewelry or accessories. You want your interviewer to be impressed by you, not by your perfume, cologne, jangly bracelets, or canary-yellow silk shirt. Once you get the job, you can see what kind of flexibility there is in dress style. But for the interview, less *is* more!

➤ MAKE A GOOD IMPRESSION

Even if you're shaking inside, there are ways at least to *appear* calm and present yourself as the best person for the job:

- Sit back in your chair with both feet flat on the floor with your hands lying comfortably in your lap. If you strive to look confident, you may well find that you actually feel confident, and this makes an impression on the interviewer.

- Always look your interviewer in the eyes. Make sure he or she has your undivided attention. Staring off into space or looking out the window may make you feel less nervous, but it certainly sends the wrong message.

- Listen carefully to your interviewer's description of the job and to any questions you're asked. Again, your interest in the job and the company will be measured by your interest in what this one person has to say.

- Pause before you answer the interviewer's questions — don't just blurt out the first thing that comes to mind. Even if the pause seems a little long to you, your reflective manner and well-thought-out answer will impress the interviewer. Still waters run deep, as they say.

- Whatever you do, leave your personal feelings about the interviewer at the door. Even if your interviewer is not someone you want for a best friend, you need to build rapport with this one person. So engage the interviewer in thoughtful discussion about the job and make sure you let it be known how intrigued you are with the job and the company. Don't be afraid to talk about how you see yourself fitting in with the company's team spirit and philosophy.

9

➤ THE INQUISITION

Once you've established rapport with your interviewer, he or she is almost certainly going to ask you questions. Each interview will get into nitty-gritty questions about the skills needed for success at the particular job offered. We can't anticipate these questions, but we can help answer three very common general questions. If you answer these well, you'll set a comfortable tone for the interview and impress the interviewer with your ability to perform under stress.

1.   "What are some of your best qualities and strengths?"

To answer this very common interview question, you should focus on how your strengths match the company's needs. Remember that your task in the interview is to keep the spotlight on the specific reasons you, and only you, are the person for the job. *Don't say:*

"I think my bouncy hair and my ability to drive a car and eat an ice cream cone at the same time are my best features."

"I'm very bossy and good at forcing other people to follow my commands."
Do say:

"I have a can-do attitude when it comes to getting challenging tasks done."

"I like the sound of the team-based approach to problem-solving at your company. I think my ability to listen to others and share in decision making would fit well with your organization."

2.   "What do you think your weaknesses are?"

Interviewers love to slip this question in since it tests your ability to think fast. Use the "weakness" question as an opportunity to show more strengths. This isn't true confession time. Your goal is to show your specific value to the company. Put a twist on this question and use it to your advantage.
Don't say:

"I have an awfully hard time getting out of bed. I don't know how I could make your 8:00 A.M. start-up time."

"I tend to make fun of my friends and family — it really drives them crazy!"

9

I think my bouncy hair and my ability to drive a car and eat an ice cream cone at the same time are my best features.

Do say:

"I'm not an early morning person on weekends, but when it comes to work, I'm at my most creative and productive during the early part of the day. In fact, I don't mind working past the last bell either."

"My sister says I'm *too much* of a perfectionist. Sometimes I just can't walk away from a problem until it's solved completely and effectively."

3.   "Where do you see yourself in five years?"

Beware here: the interviewer does not want to know that you've always wanted to live in Cleveland or Phoenix, or that you hanker to sail to Tahiti. The interviewer wants to know if you have realistic career goals that mesh with the company's view of growth potential for the particular job you're interviewing for.

9

Don't say:

"I see myself as CEO of a large multinational corporation."

"I'll probably move to Australia with my brother in two years. He's starting an ostrich farm there."

Do say:

"I want to be on a learning and growth track in this company. There are so many interesting facets of this job. I want to understand as much as I can about the way this company works so well and productively."

"In a few years I want to be in a position where I teach other people about the benefits of the team approach. I want to be a team leader sharing my skills and supporting other team members' development."

If you can handle these three questions, chances are that you will have passed a major hurdle in the interview process. Keep in mind that this is your chance to promote your strengths—no one else can put in a good word for you at this stage. Make the most of this chance and *speak up for yourself*.

[EFFECTIVE TELEPHONE SKILLS]

Using the telephone in business is another skill closely tied to the speech-making skills you've learned in earlier chapters. Few business skills are more important than using the telephone effectively. Nothing is more irksome to a caller than someone who does not use the telephone well, who sounds fake or phony (no pun intended!) or uninterested in the caller. Each company has its own telephone guidelines, but there are some general rules of thumb when it comes to handling basic phone transactions. We'll cover three areas: answering the phone, screening calls, and using the hold button. Of course the most important rule is to be courteous and polite—but what does this really mean? The following list gives you some specific pointers on phone use:

➤ ANSWERING THE PHONE

1. Smile when you pick up the phone. Sounds crazy, maybe, but the person on the other line can hear the smile in your voice.

9

Smile when you pick up the phone.

2. Say hello and state your name and your department or place of business.

3. Be enthusiastic—don't sound as if the *last* thing you want to do is help someone.

4. Don't gush. It's a big turnoff when someone answers with a syrupy-sweet greeting. It's always better to be yourself on the phone.

Don't say:

"What do ya want?"

"I'm really busy now. Can you speed it up?"

"Hello, this is Jeff Brownstone. I am so delighted you called Acme Supply. How can I be of superior service to you today, valued customer?"

Do say:

"Hello, this is Katherine Schwartz in reception. Can I help you?"

"Good morning, Brian Jones speaking."

9

➤ SCREENING CALLS

Screening calls for someone else is a real skill. You may be asked to screen calls for a supervisor or a colleague. Here too, be as courteous as you can (without sounding fake). After all, no one likes to be screened, but most callers recognize the necessity of this practice.

1.   Answer the phone politely and enthusiastically. Don't make the caller feel that you resent the call as an intrusion.

2.   Tell the caller that you'll see if your colleague is available.

3.   Don't ask the caller the nature of her call—this is too much of a tip-off that the call is being screened.

4.   If you know that your supervisor can't be interrupted, let the caller know right away that he or she is unavailable at the moment but will return the call later.

Don't say:

"May I ask who's calling and the nature of your business? I'll see if Ms. Johnson is available."

"She's talking to people from the human relations department today. Why don't you try on Thursday—I know she won't want to talk to you now."

Do say:

"He's on the other line now. May I take your name and number and ask him to get back to you? Thanks for calling."

"Katherine is in a meeting this morning. Can she get back to you, or is there some way I can help you?"

➤ USING THE HOLD BUTTON

Putting people on hold is another skill requiring a graceful phone manner. Face it, most callers *hate* being put on hold—who knows when they'll be let out of telephone purgatory? What you can do, through your skill and manner, is ease the caller's trauma.

1.   Tell the caller he or she will be on hold for just a moment, and try to be truthful about this. If you know that the hold will be much longer, state this and either take a message or

suggest that the caller phone back at a less busy time (tell the caller a good time to call).

2.   Never, never, never, switch the caller onto hold without stating your intention. If your supervisor is buzzing you, or you have another call coming in, don't just press the hold button on call one to address call two. Nobody likes to be rudely cut off.

3.   When you're bringing someone back from hold, be as polite as you can, and apologize for the delay. Callers appreciate your understanding that they, too, are busy and would rather not spend time floating on hold.

Don't say:
    "I don't have time for you now. Wait on hold until I do."
    "I'm putting you on hold now. No, I can't take your message."
Do say:
    "Would you mind holding for a moment? Or may I take a message and get back to you?"
    "I'm sorry, but I need to put you on hold for just a minute — I promise!"

[SPECIAL OCCASIONS]

At some point in your life, you may be asked to introduce a speaker, or you may be offered an award. How would you handle these special occasions? Chances are, you might get nervous and distressed, nervous and elated, or maybe just nervous and nervous. There are no stock phrases that every speaker should use in these situations, but we can give you some general guidelines.

➤ MAKING INTRODUCTIONS

1.   Keep your introductory comments relevant to the occasion. If the speaker you're introducing is talking about a recent trip to the rain forests of Central America, tell the audience a bit about the speaker's background in conservation and travel. You needn't

9

describe the speaker's other hobbies, politics, or family life. Although these items may be interesting in and of themselves (or they may not be!), they are irrelevant to the speech topic.

2.   Keep your comments *brief.* Observe the cardinal rule: stop talking before the audience wants to stop listening. In other words, your role as the introducer is to whet the audience's appetite for the real speech to follow. Don't drag the introduction on for so long that the audience wants to leave before the main event.

3.   Tell the audience why they will want to sit up and pay attention. One of your tasks is to get the audience involved in the speech topic. Give the audience some clear reasons *why* the speech will be useful, informative, or just entertaining. For the rain forest speech, you might tell the audience that just by listening they will gain unique insights on the highs and lows of women traveling alone. Or you could say that the speech will make them take another look at the world's ecosystems and what can be done to preserve them.

4.   Keep in the background. Don't try to switch the spotlight on yourself. Not only is this confusing to the audience (they may wonder who is the featured speaker), but it's just plain irritating to everybody.

➤ ACCEPTING AWARDS OR HONORS

Although your friends may always have told you how great you were, there will come a time when someone else, an instructor, a supervisor, or a colleague, formally recognizes what your friends saw all along. When you are given an award or honor, you'll need to thank the people who have recognized you, and say a few words.

1.   Be brief. No one wants to listen to a long list of all the people you've ever worked with on a project, or listen to the names of every teacher you've had since the first grade. A general (and genuine) comment is a gracious way of including many people who have helped you and will eliminate the chance of forgetting one name. "I'd like to thank all my good friends, relatives, and colleagues who offered support and guidance over the years" is

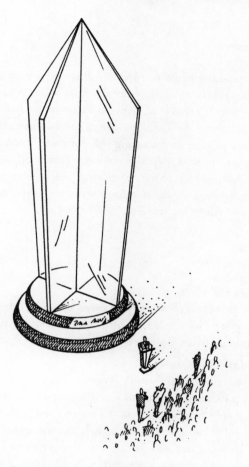

*I'd like to thank
all of the people
who have sup-
ported me...*

better than "I want to thank my husband, my mother, Mrs. Jones, the mailman, my third grade science teacher, my dog, my cat . . . ."
2.   Make connections. Most people in the audience will be interested in what this particular award means to you at this time in your life. You'll have reasons why the award is significant and why it's been a goal (if it has). For instance, Academy Award winners might tell the audience that the award they just won marks their acceptance into the Hollywood mainstream. An employee of the year winner might tell her colleagues that she feels ready to move on to the next level of training, and the award gives her the confidence to take the next step.

9

☞   *Summary*

All the speaking skills you learn will serve you on a daily basis —
at work, at school, with your friends, with your family. With
practice, you'll build confidence and get to enjoy communicating
in all situations. As social creatures, people spend a good deal of
their lives talking and sharing information. Look at interviews,
telephone time, and special occasions as more opportunities to put
your speaking skills to use. Speaking well is, of course, one of the
best ways you can show others what's unique and interesting
about *you.* Jump in, and *speak up for yourself!*

☞   *Skill Builders*

1.   Act the Part.
    With a class partner, take turns being an interviewer and an
applicant for a job. Ask each other the common types of questions
that come up in an interview and brainstorm effective responses.

2.   Play Telephone.
    Use your imagination to create a hypothetical company that
offers a particular service to its customers. Choose one person to
play the role of receptionist. Class members should take turns
"calling" this receptionist with various requests. The whole class
could then discuss ways to handle the series of calls. Adapt the
telephone techniques described in the chapter, and come up with
your own strategies.

3.   Just Desserts.
    Give an "award" to one member of the class. This student
should then deliver an impromptu (but gracious and brief) acceptance speech. Take turns around the classroom so everyone gets
a moment in the sun!

SUGGESTED

TOPICS

FOR

SPEECHES

I.   The one-point speech

- My worst fear about speech class.
- My favorite ethnic food.
- The first time my child spoke.
- The best job I ever had.
- The worst job I ever had.
- The best book I have read, and why.
- My all-time favorite movie, and why.
- Why I chose my course of study.
- My favorite outdoor activity.
- The best conversation I had with a neighbor.
- The worst car I ever owned.
- The best car I ever owned.
- My first date.
- My worst date.
- Why the city is the best place to live.
- The benefits of living in the country.
- My best date.
- A great fishing spot, and why.
- My most embarrassing moment.
- The best way to clean an apartment—fast!
- The ups and downs of being a working student.
- My favorite coffee blend.
- The best way to get across town in rush-hour traffic.

II.   The speech to inform

- Members of my family.
- My two or three favorite pets.

- Three jobs I hate most.

- The three best jobs I ever had.

- Name two musical albums and tell why they are your favorites.

- Two or three happy holidays (Christmas, Halloween, Passover, etc.).

- Share interesting traditions of your family or religious groups.

- Describe special characteristics of the various neighborhoods in your city.

- Analyze several of the main differences of philosophy between the Democrat and Republican parties.

- If you find yourself in trouble with the Internal Revenue Service, here are three steps you can take to try to get out of it.

- Talk to three generations of your family and share their differing views on modern morality.

- Explain the procedure for getting a driver's license.

- Present your views on environmental protection, defining the problem and briefly presenting a solution.

III. The demonstration speech

- Show how to prepare:
A pancake breakfast for a hungry family.
Your favorite ethnic food.
The recipe that's been handed down for generations in your family.
A nutritious snack that even a fussy teenager would accept.
- Show how to operate a camera.
- Demonstrate the latest dance steps (it would help if you had a partner and something upon which to play music).
- Demonstrate several aerobic exercises and explain the purpose of each.
- Show how to change a tire.

- Demonstrate the easiest way to keep kids busy on a car trip.
- Demonstrate the Heimlich maneuver and several CPR methods.
- Show how to bathe, diaper, and clothe a small baby.
- Demonstrate sports techniques, such as those used in basketball or soccer.
- Demonstrate (gently) karate or other martial arts skills.
- Show how to re-pot a plant.
- Show what should be included in a car's winter survival kit.
- Show how to trim a child's hair.

IV. The persuasive speech (Take either the pro or con argument, but remember that no negative words can be used in the proposition.)

    A.   Proposition of policy.
        *1. Everyone should go on to further education immediately after graduating from high school.
         2. It would be best to work a year or two after high school before pursuing advanced education.

        *1. Instructors should spend more time in their offices to be available to students.
         2. Students should arrange their schedules to accommodate the instructors.

        *1. This institution should establish a uniform student dress code.
         2. This institution should allow students to dress however they choose.

        *1. The United States government should allow a woman to choose if she wants an abortion.
         2. The government should have a law that prohibits abortion.

    B.   Proposition of value
        *1. It is better to live in school-owned housing while attending college than to live in an apartment.

2.   It is better to live off-campus while in college than in school-owned housing.

*1.   It is better to work part-time than to plan to devote most of your time to studying.
2.   It is better to spend your time studying than to have the burden of a job.

*1.   It is better for students to remain single all through their education than to be married while attending school.
2.   It is better (with the right person) to be married while in school than to be single.

C.   Proposition of fact
*1.   Capital punishment is a deterrent against a violent crime.
2.   Capital punishment should never be allowed because it has no effect on future criminal behavior.

*1.   I will prove to you that the U.S. Postal Service gives very little service for a lot of money.
2.   I will prove to you that the U.S. Postal Service is the best bargain in the country.

*1.   I will prove that the Gulf War (against Iraq in 1991) was justified and was ended at the right time.
2.   The Gulf War was political in nature and the United States had no business being in it.

*1.   I am going to prove that the current president of the United States is the best one we could have for this time in history.
2.   The current president is the worst person we could have for this time in history.

[
SAMPLE

SPEECHES
]

Each of these speeches follows the format of one of the speech types described in the text.

[SPEECH 1:   ONE-POINT INFORMATIVE]

Man next door and I look upon one another with suspicion. He's a raker and a shoveler, as I see it. A troubler of the natural ways of the earth. Left over from the breed that conquered the wilderness. He thinks of me in simpler terms: lazy.

See, every week during the fall he's out raking little leaves into piles. And every time it snows, he's out tormenting the white stuff with his shovel. Once, out of either eagerness or outrage, he even managed to shovel a heavy frost. "Can't let old Mother Nature get ahead of you," says he.

So I tell him he hasn't the sense God gave a stump. In a kind of careful way. Leaves have been falling down for thousands and thousands of years, I tell him. And the earth did pretty well before rakes and people, I tell him. Old Mother Nature put the leaves where she wanted them and they made more earth. We need more earth, I tell him. We're running out of it, I tell him. And snow — snow is not my enemy, I tell him. Snow is God's way of telling people to slow down and rest and stay in bed for a day. And besides, snow always solves itself. Mixes with the leaves to form more earth, I tell him.

His yard does look neat, I must admit —*if* neatness is important. And he didn't fall down getting to his car last snowtime, and I in fact did. And he is a good neighbor, even if he is a raker and a shoveler. I'm open-minded about this thing.

Still, my yard has a Oriental carpet of red and yellow and green and brown. And his doesn't. And I spent the same time he spent shoveling snow collecting it in bottles to mix with orange juice July next, and I taped the sound of it falling and then used the tape to wrap Christmas presents (*snow has lots of uses*).

I gave him a bottle of vintage winter snow for Christmas, wrapped in some of that tape. He gave me a rake. We're giving each other lessons in the proper use of these tools. I think he's got no religion, and I'm trying to convert him. He thinks I've got too much, and he's trying to get me to back off.

But in the end, in the final end of it all — I win. For he and I — and even you — will become what the leaves and snow become, and go where the leaves and snow go — whether we rake or shovel or not.

From *All I Really Need to Know I Learned in Kindergarten* by Robert Fulghum. Copyright © 1986, 1988 by Robert Fulghum. Reprinted by permission of Villard Books, a division of Random House, Inc.

[SPEECH 2: PERSUASIVE PROPOSITION OF FACT]

Friends and fellow citizens: — I stand before you to-night under indictment for the alleged crime of having voted at the last presidential election, without having a lawful right to vote. It shall be my work this evening to prove to you that in thus voting, I not only committed no crime, but, instead, simply exercised my *citizen's rights*, guaranteed to me and all United States citizens by the National Constitution, beyond the power of any State to deny.

The preamble of the Federal Constitution says:

"We the people of the United States, in order to form a more perfect union, establish justice, insure *domestic* tranquillity, provide for the common defense, promote the general welfare, and secure the blessings of liberty to ourselves and our posterity, do ordain and establish this Constitution for the United States of America."

It was we, the people, not we, the white male citizens; nor yet we, the male citizens; but we, the whole people, who formed the Union. And we formed it, not to give the blessings of liberty, but to secure them; not to the half of ourselves and the half of our posterity, but to the whole people — women as well as men. And it is a downright mockery to talk to women of their enjoyment of the blessings of liberty while they are denied the use of the only means of securing them provided by this democratic-republican government — the ballot.

For any State to make sex a qualification that must ever result in the disfranchisement of one entire half of the people is to pass a bill of attainder, or an *ex post facto* law, and is therefore a violation of the supreme law of the land. By it the blessings of liberty are for ever withheld from women and their female posterity. To them this government has no just powers derived from the consent of the governed. To them this government is not a democracy. It is not a republic. It is an odious aristocracy; a hateful oligarchy of sex; the most hateful aristocracy ever established on the face of the globe; an oligarchy of wealth, where the rich govern the poor. An oligarchy of learning, where the educated govern the ignorant, or even an oligarchy of race, where the Saxon rules the African, might be endured; but this oligarchy of sex, which makes father, brothers, husband, sons, the oligarchs over the mother and sisters, the wife and daughters of every household—which ordains all men sovereigns, all women subjects, carries dissension, discord and rebellion into every home of the nation.

Webster, Worcester and Bouvier all define a citizen to be a person in the United States, entitled to vote and hold office.

The only question left to be settled now is: Are women persons? And I hardly believe any of our opponents will have the hardihood to say they are not. Being persons, then, women are citizens; and no State has a right to make any law, or to enforce any old law, that shall abridge their privileges or immunities. Hence, every discrimination against women in the constitutions and laws of the several States is to-day null and void, precisely as in every one against negroes.

Susan B. Anthony, "On Woman's Right to Suffrage," from *The World's Great Speeches*, Edited by Lewis Copeland & Lawrence W. Lamm (New York: Dover Publications, Inc., 1973), p. 321.

[SPEECH 3:   PERSUASIVE PROPOSITION OF VALUE]

. . . Today the expenditure of billions of dollars every year on weapons acquired for the purpose of making sure we never need them is essential to the keeping of peace. But surely the acquisition of such idle stockpiles—which can only destroy and can never create—is not the only, much less the most efficient, means of assuring peace.

I speak of peace, therefore, as the necessary rational end of rational men. I realize the pursuit of peace is not as dramatic as the pursuit of war—and frequently the words of the pursuer fall on deaf ears. But we have no more urgent task.

Some say that it is useless to speak of peace or world law or world disarmament—and that it will be useless until the leaders of the Soviet Union adopt a more enlightened attitude. I hope they do. I believe we can help them do it.

But I also believe that we must re-examine our own attitudes—as individuals and as a nation—for our attitude is as essential as theirs. And every graduate of this school, every thoughtful citizens who despairs of war and wishes to bring peace, should begin by looking inward—by examining his own attitude toward the course of the cold war and towards freedom and peace here at home.

First: Examine our attitude towards peace itself. Too many of us think it is impossible. Too many think it is unreal. But that is a dangerous, defeatist belief. It leads to the conclusion that war is inevitable—that mankind is doomed—that we are gripped by forces we cannot control.

We need not accept that view. Our problems are man-made. Therefore they can be solved by man. And man can be as big as he wants. No problem of human destiny is beyond human beings. Man's reason and spirit have often solved the seemingly unsolvable—and we believe they can do it again.

I am not referring to the absolute, infinite concepts of universal peace and goodwill of which some fantasies and fanatics dream. I do not deny the value of hopes and dreams but we merely invite discouragement and incredulity by making that our only and immediate goal.

Let us focus instead on a more practical, more attainable peace—based not on a sudden revolution in human nature but on a gradual evolution in human institutions—on a series of concrete actions and effective agreements which are in the interests of all concerned.

There is no single, simple key to this peace—no grand or magic formula to be adopted by one or two powers. Genuine peace must be the product of many nations, the sum of many acts. It must be dynamic, not static, changing to meet the challenge of each new generation. For each is a process—a way of solving problems.

With such a peace, there will still be quarrels and conflicting interests, as there are within families and nations. World peace, like community peace, does not require that each man love his neighbor—it requires only that they live together with mutual tolerance, submitting their disputes to a just and peaceful settlement. And history teaches us that enmities between nations, as between individuals, do not last forever. However fixed our likes and dislikes may seem, the tide of time and events will often bring surprising changes in the relations between nations and neighbors.

So let us persevere. Peace need not be impracticable—war need not be manageable and less remote—we can help all people to see it, to draw hope from it, and to move irresistibly towards it.

John F. Kennedy, excerpt from "The Strategy of Peace," from *The World's Great Speeches*. Lewis Copeland & Lawrence W. Lamm, eds. (New York: Dover Publications, Inc., 1973), p. 742.

[SPEECH 4: PERSUASIVE SPEECH]

... Like most people in my generation, I was brought up to believe in progress. I still do. But we're at a point where we have to ask our-selves if we are the beneficiaries of our progress, or the victims? Manifest destiny doesn't work anymore. Progress from now on has to mean something different. We are running out of places, we're running out of the resources, and we're running out of time.

Scientists tell us the struggle to sustain life in this earth's environment could be won in the next decade, or lost. As we approach the year 2000, we've now heard the hard facts.

Over 100 million people, half of our population, already breathe air that is unhealthy.

Health experts tell us not to eat the fish from our own rivers, lakes, and oceans.

We've got chemical and nuclear wastes piling up at dump sites and leeching into our land and water.

Our oceans are warming, our ozone layer's got a hole that's getting bigger and, according to Carl Sagan, a whole football field of rain forests are vanishing — not every hour, not every minute, but every second? With each tick, a field of trees are gone.

It's a pretty lousy legacy we've left for our children. We should be apologizing.

Native Americans try to live with seven generations in mind. Recently we have been plunging ahead blindly, without plans for even one generation.

The environmental movement has been growing for over 20 years, and in the seventies, it seemed for a while the Government was responding, passing regulations, supporting research for things like alternative fuels. Some corporations came up with energy plans, and some discovered conservation is good business. But today, when people in every community put more and more concern into the environment, the government in Washington seems to treat it as just one more special interest to be appeased.

What happened? There was so much good work done in the seventies. Where did we go off track? In the eighties, we had an executive branch whose major policy seemed to be to set loose banking, housing, real estate, energy — to fast-buck kings with a minimum of regulations. What a step backwards!

The results have been catastrophic. I think for the environment, there's never been such a time of naked greed and exploitations as we have seen in the last decade. The damage done, we'll feel for a long time.

The Reagan administration filled key appointments with agents of private profit who were put in place to sell off or pay out public assets. There seemed to be a mean-spirited attitude behind them. Their idea of land use policy was just more real estate development. James Watt, Ann Burford, Rita LaValle, Samuel Pierce, all foxes guarding the chicken coop.

When the occasional critic got up to ask if something was going wrong, the strategy was to give a superior little chuckle and dismiss the "prophets of gloom and doom, running down America."

Well, I'm not a prophet of gloom and doom. I've always assumed love of land and love of country go together. I think I'm like a lot of other people who are tired of being humored and handled.

A high-water mark for trying to sucker the voters came during the 1988 campaign. No wonder so many Americans stayed home and didn't vote. The big issue we were always hearing about was who was most effective at manipulating the public.

So instead of policy-makers you hire image-makers. You create some backdrop like a Salem cigarette ad and you announce, "I'm an environmentalist!"

We all remember that famous Bush-for-President ad with sewage pipes emptying into Boston Harbor. But after the election, who was watching when the administration cut $400 million from funds to do the job?

When the President was campaigning and was pressed on global warming and the greenhouse effect, he said, "Wait till you see the White House effect!" We've seen it: it's a call for more study. Well, that's an old stall.

... We can't wait around anymore for solutions to come from the top. It isn't going to happen. And as for Congress, the action there is too late, too slow, and too full of compromise.

American democracy has a long history of change won by popular movements: women's suffrage, labor laws, the civil rights movement, the end of the Vietnam War. It seems to me the grassroots activism we see around the country is evidence that there is a movement underway that wants action on behalf of the environment.

What we're living with is the result of human choices. And it can be changed by making better, wiser choices. As we've learned in the past, the media can play an important role in these events. I hope the work continues.

Robert Redford, at the National Press Club, Washington, D.C., from *The Reference Shelf, Representative American Speeches 1990–1991*. Edited by Owen Peterson (New York: H.W. Wilson Company, 1991), p. 52. Reprinted by permission of Robert Redford and the Sundance Group.

[SELECTED

BIBLIOGRAPHY]

➤ COMMUNICATION THEORY

Benson, Thomas W. *American Rhetoric, Context and Criticism.*
    Carbondale: Southern Illinois University Press, 1989.
Burns, James H. *Speak for Yourself: An Introduction to Public
    Speaking.* New York: Random House, 1981.
Humes, James C. *Roles Speakers Play.* New York: Harper &
    Row, 1976.
Douglas Ehninger, et al. eds. *Principles and Types of Speech
    Communication.* 9th ed. Glenview: Scott, Foresman and
    Company, 1982.

➤ OVERCOMING STAGE FRIGHT

Hoff, Ron. *"I Can See You Naked," A Fearless Guide to Making Great
    Presentations.* Kansas City: Andrews & McMeel, 1988.
Nelson, Robert B. *Louder And Funnier/A Practical Guide for
    Overcoming Stagefright in Speechmaking.* Berkeley: Ten Speed
    Press, 1985.
Osgood, Charles. *Osgood on Speaking—How to Think on Your Feet
    Without Falling on Your Face.* New York: William Morrow
    & Co., Inc., 1988.
Rogers, Natalie H. *Talk-Power, How to Speak without Fear: A
    Systematic Training Program.* New York: Dodd, Mead &
    Co., 1982.
Sarnoff, Dorothy. *Never Be Nervous Again: The World-Renowned
    Speech Expert Reveals Her Time-Tested Method for Foolproof
    Control of Nervousness in Communicating Situations.* New
    York: Crown Publishers, Inc., 1987.
Triplett, Robert. *Stagefright, Letting It Work for You.* Chicago:
    Nelson-Hall, 1983.
Wydro, Kenneth. *Think on Your Feet, The Art of Thinking &
    Speaking under Pressure.* Englewood Cliffs: Prentice-Hall,
    Inc., 1981.

➤ IMPROVING SPEECH-MAKING SKILLS IN THE BUSINESS ARENA

Berg, Karen, and Andrew Gilman. *Get to the Point. How to Say
    What You Mean and Get What You Want.* Toronto: Bantam
    Books, 1989.

Carnegie, Dale. *How to Develop Self-Confidence & Influence People by Public Speaking.* New York: Simon & Schuster, 1956.

Frank, Milo. *How to Get Your Point Across in 30 Seconds — or Less.* New York: Simon & Schuster, 1986.

Hamlin, Sonya. *How to Talk so People Listen: The Real Key to Job Success.* New York: Harper & Row, 1988.

Peoples, David. *Presentations Plus — David Peoples' Proven Techniques.* New York: John Wiley & Sons, 1988.

Robinson, James W. *Better Speeches in 10 Simple Steps.* Rocklin: Prima Publishing and Communications, 1989.

➤ HUMOR IN SPEECHES

Iapoce, Michael. *"A Funny Thing Happened on the Way to the Board Room" — Using Humor in Business Speaking.* New York: John Wiley & Sons, Inc., 1988.

Perret, Gene. *Using Humor for Effective Business Speaking.* New York: Sterling Publishing Co., Inc., 1989.

Prochnow, Herbert V., and Herbert V. Prochnow, Jr., eds. *The Public Speaker's Treasure Chest.* 4th ed. New York: Harper & Row Publishers, 1986.

➤ QUOTATIONS FOR SPEECHES

Fitzhenry, Robert I., ed. *Barnes & Noble Book of Quotations.* New York: Barnes & Noble, 1981.

Fadiman, Clifton, ed. *The Little, Brown Book of Anecdotes.* Boston: Little, Brown Co., 1985.

Kent, Robert W., ed. *Money Talks — The 3000 Greatest Quotes on Business from Aristotle to DeLorean.* New York: Facts on File, 1985.

Conlin, Joseph R., ed. *The Morrow Book of Quotations in American History.* New York: William Morrow & Co., Inc., 1984.

Gross, John, ed. *The Oxford Book of Aphorisms.* Oxford: Oxford University Press, 1983.

Peter, Dr. Laurence J. *Peter's Quotations. Ideas for Our Time.* New York: Bantam Books, 1979.

[INDEX]